ANCHORED

Closing Life-Challenge

Discover how becoming Anchored and Living Anchored thru the Closing Life-Challenge experienced by this group of successful seniors called the Oaks, who are living a legacy of love and prayer cause enduring change in hearts and community.

Novel by Janice R Hunt.

Print ISBN: 978-1-64719-254-9
Epub ISBN: 978-1-64719-255-6
Mobi ISBN: 978-1-64719-256-3

Published by BookLocker.com, Inc., St. Petersburg, Florida.

Printed on acid-free paper.

The characters and events in this book are fictitious. Any similarity to real persons, living or dead, is coincidental and not intended by the author.

Scriptures marked KJV are taken from the KING JAMES VERSION (KJV): KING JAMES VERSION, public domain. All scripture is from the King James Version of the Bible, unless otherwise noted.

Scriptures marked NAS are taken from the NEW AMERICAN STANDARD (NAS): Scripture taken from the NEW AMERICAN STANDARD BIBLE®, copyright© 1960, 1962, 1963, 1968, 1971, 1972, 1973, 1975, 1977, 1995 by The Lockman Foundation. Used by permission. Scripture from the New American Standard Bible are noted.

BookLocker.com, Inc.
2021

First Edition

Library of Congress Cataloguing in Publication Data
Hunt, Janice R
ANCHORED: Closing Life-Challenge by Janice R Hunt
Library of Congress Control Number: 2021904718

This is a work of fiction; some have called allegorical like.

References to warrior and warfare, battle, battlefield, and Valliant Warrior, etc., are of a spiritual nature.

An abundant thank you goes to my husband, 3 sons and 3 daughters-in-law and 5 grandchildren. Your lives are worthy of praise; however, your humility will take no pleasure.

References to teachers James Everette Weeks and Etta Mae Dunn Weeks are used with permission of their daughter, Nancy Weeks Vaughn.

Suzanne Mauer's story of traditional Hawaiian Hanai adoption was used with Suzanne's permission.

Many characters are inspired from passionate aged leaders, who are still fulfilling their purpose in life. Their names have been changed.

Author owns copyright of this fiction novel, as well as illustrations created by John Collado and photos created by Camera Works.

This American historical Christian fiction work is suitable for young adult 12-18, and older.

May God be glorified.

"A life without God is like a boat without an anchor." Billy Graham

Author website: https://janicehuntauthor.com/

Foreword

It is absurd to suppose a newborn baby is left in the care of an ageless but frail crew of elderly residents in an assisted living residence.

Suppose these residents have felt no longer useful yet have a wealth of experience and knowledge, with no purpose in life.

Suppose the individuals have longed for one *Closing Life-Challenge*. The battle is on: The Parenting Paradox.

As though peering through the lattice, and observing these events firsthand, the accounts were delivered to me by none other than the 'Valiant Warrior', The Reverend Gideon.

This novel is not a preachy diatribe, but a demonstration of lives lived with biblical purpose, extending grace in undeserved places.

Charity Grace Gideon, narrator

ANCHORED:

Closing Life-Challenge

Janice R. Hunt

Table of Contents

CHAPTER ONE
The Closer

"Gid!"

"Dr. Lucas."

After a cordial handshake, their eyes met in mutual respect and admiration. "Gid," said Dr. Lucas, "you will remember? We talked about the day...?"

Gid did remember. He sat in that same hard chair on that day, in Dr. Lucas' office gazing through the window at the Oak trees down in the River Park with his mate Purah of 50 plus years, at his side—rubbing his swollen fingers. "Gideon, you have overcome some of the common health obstacles of being African American, but this time the odds are weighted against you," commented Dr. Lucas.

Gids eyes had once again strayed to Harbor Oaks River Park.

Dr. Lucas continued, "...the day that I would refer you back to your maker. There really isn't anything at this stage medically to be done, except keep you comfortable, and attempt to control symptoms. There won't be any more hospitalizations. Gid, I will order a nurse to come to your house."

Harbor Oaks World

Reverend Gideon[1] was not a stranger to the medical settings. Not only did he spend countless hours with his ill friends and local church folks, of late, he had spent numerous sessions in the hospital with his own Congestive Heart Failure. Walking to his doctor visits had become an arduous chore.

The Reverend Gideon, once an imposing presence, now sockless, shoes untied, and in a daze, found himself alone under the beloved oak grove, down by the river, crying out to God. "Um, um, um, how did I get here? Lord, I guess I will be seeing you soon." Struggling to get a breath, "It's been a long war."

Hearing himself breathe, Gideon exhaled with slow weightiness.

Comforts from childhood came, being there on the oak-canopied riverbank, with the gentle breeze in his face, the fragrance of the lemon verbena mingled with the river smells, and that sound of almost ceaseless praying filtering through the trees.

In harmony, those cherished sights and odors satisfied his frequent longing to hear the captain's cry, "Cast your nets to the other side," Jn 21:6[2], then, a bizarre silence. *The Spirit of God is still hovering over the watery deep" Gen 1:1[3], thought Gid.*

Over there it is, thought Gid, *in the mist, that tattered old ship. Oh, how it weathers the storms. The timbers are scarred and worn. Yet, it is forever here, now—in my present.*

Painfully, Gid inhaled with purpose and determination. *I heard that call so many years ago, now. It came for me, when I was an energetic young college student. That call is as fresh as ever. As long as I live, I will be casting my net for men.*

---

[1] ((King James Version) n.d.) (Inspiration for character Judges 6)
[2] ((KJV) n.d.)
[3] ((KJV) author's paraphrase n.d.)

"Gideon, I have one more engagement for you, one more battle, one *Closing Life-Challenge*."

Looking around, Gid was sure the Lord was right beside him.

Gid placed his hand on his chest. "That feeling is here again, like an enlivening stimulant."

Gideon's heart was vibrating.

"Gideon, this battle will be the most noted battle of your life."

"It will demonstrate the significance of leaving a living legacy, that will bring to others a fountainhead of comfort and grace. You will receive your orders soon."

Shaking out his long white handkerchief, "Lord, but this warrior is tired. Some of the battles have not been won, Lord. I am distracted and weak."

"Gideon, you are a valiant warrior. You have diligently demonstrated your faith in the heat of battle."

"Yes, Lord, I know my time is short and my body is worn out, but I still have so much love and experience to pass on."

Weeping, "Lord, I wonder if we don't know who or what we are, until we are faced with our final call?" Wrapping his handkerchief around his swollen hand, he swiped it across his face.

Longing to linger, he turned to leave. Gid felt a cool breeze kicking up. "Lord, walking is a struggle now; the shortness of breath makes me so fatigued. This old, scarred battleship is dragging my anchor feet around with no steam to go ahead."

"Gideon, I will be your strength."

Taking another step, "Doc Lucas said I could smother, if I lie down. You know. I have been sleeping in my recliner for months." Gideon struggled to reach the bench beside the whitewashed tree.

"Gideon, you have diligently taught on grace and mercy. You will experience my grace the same tomorrow, as yesterday and today."

"Yes, Lord. I believe with my whole being."

The towering Harbor Oaks began to sway in the breeze, as Gid began plodding his way back to his assisted living apartment. He could smell the rain coming. Rain began pouring down in sheets, stinging his face, and yet he kept his feeble stride.

Thoughts of his past spiritual battles were rumbling in his head. Battle by battle, God had shown himself faithful to Gid. He had led so many wayward souls into the safe harbor of a loving, forgiving God. Gid kept repeating, "Orders soon?"

His counsel to friends suffering financial loss had strengthened their integrity and allowed them to remain honorable in their business deals.

Prayers, oh the prayers, for wayward children, mothers seeking abortion, a dad in prison—restored to family…!

Pastoring his childhood friends presented new challenges every day. Helping carry those heavy burdens was always a walk of faith.

"Lord, this little town is our mooring. You have allowed our neighbors to live here a lifetime, and with short commutes, we have all managed successful careers."

Shaking his head, "Moving into this complex turned out to be just what we all needed. Our bodies are riddled with aging processes that are debilitating—with Purah's arthritis, and compression fractures, and my CHF. The two of us could no longer manage day to day. Everything here is designed for the handicapped." He chuckled.

"Oh, but thank you, Jesus, you have allowed us to keep our mental faculties. There are others whose cognition is failing. Lord, why us? We just can't praise you enough. Lord, you have been our lighthouse."

Purah, standing on the stoop as he approached said, "Gideon, our *crew* is out looking everywhere for you. They knew you had walked to your appointment. They don't need to be out in this downpour any more than you."

Just as she had finished lovingly scolding him, Miller, Maude, and Ochre came hobbling and staggering in behind him, drenched.

Maude, shaking her hands from the dripping rain, "While I drove through the neighborhood, Miller was praying like a wild man."

"Oh, yeah, I heard him, down on the riverbank," said Gid.

"The neighbors were coming out on their porches to see what the ruckus was. Miller knows how difficult it is for you to walk anyway these days, Gid." Giving him a hug, "Oh, we are so thankful that you are okay. Why Gid! Your clothes aren't even wet," said Maude.

Ochre chimed in, "There isn't a dry thread on any of us and look at you. Turn around. I don't know what to make of this—you can barely creep along."

Maude, snuff in lip, walked around him in a circle, then while stepping back, all the while staring at him, she pondered this oddity. Under her breath she muttered, "Nobody but you, Gid."

Gid added, "Well, you did say 'Miller was praying like a wild man'. I guess he got through."

Facing Gid, Miller placed his right hand on Gid's shoulder and his frail left arm, practically mummified on Gid's arm. As he squeezed Gid's shoulder, "I just thank God, you made it back, and you are okay," Miller said.

They all laughed in bewilderment and then made their way out, leaving puddles behind.

Miller was an old cowboy who took God at His word. Everything stood black and white to him.

Ochre said, "Miller, you look like that limping fellar on TV."

While making their way home Maude was thinking, *our saintly old schoolteacher taught Miller the value of prayer. His family was sharecroppers, back during the Great Depression. He saw his daddy being led to the Lord by that tenacious teacher. Mr. Weeks[4] poured himself into us boys and girls. To this day, we are bonded together like brothers and sisters. The power of prayer was established in Miller's heart through those formative years, and he learned how to love others through his prayers.*

As Purah began mopping water, she said, "Gid, this one will take some explaining."

Gideon preoccupied with his recent encounter, "I remember the story in the Bible about the fleece being dry, with dew on the ground around it. Huh, *I am* totally dry. I'll have to look that one up."

"What *is* God about to do, Gid?"

Studying, "Baby, just maybe that dry fleece is something to do with my visit from the Lord, just now, at the oak grove, at Harbor Oaks River Park. He impressed on my heart, 'I have one more engagement for you; one more battle, one *Closing Life-Challenge*. This battle will be the most noted battle of your life and will demonstrate the importance of leaving a living legacy, that will birth a fountainhead of comfort and grace. You will receive your orders soon.'"

"Purah, God called me a 'Valiant Warrior.'"

"Okay, baby, let's begin dressing for the Wednesday evening worship." Purah wondered, *whatever could 'another battle' mean? Gideon is so frail. Just feeding himself takes all his energy.*

"Gid, baby, if anyone knows you have been a 'valiant warrior,' I surely do. Do you remember the time you got arrested for speeding?"

---

[4] (James Everette Weeks, Sr. October 03, 1906; June 13, 2001)

Chuckling, Gid replied, "I sure do."

"That young woman called you from the abortion clinic to come get her. She was scared and alone. You had been counseling with her to give birth to her baby."

"How could I ever forget that?" said Gid.

"You went flying out of that wedding reception like your pants were on fire. You didn't any more get out of town when you got stopped for speeding." By this time, Purah was laughing out loud. "They thought you were drinking and arrested you."

"Yeah, once they realized what was going on, I was given a police escort all the way to that abortion clinic, sixty miles away."

"Yes, Gid, you are a 'valiant warrior.' You are the 'righteousness of God' 2 Cor 5:21[5], in Christ!"

Gid, shaking his head as a tear escaped, "Um, um, um."

"Purah, baby, let's drive tonight. I don't believe I can walk and then preach."

---

[5] ((KJV) n.d.)

CHAPTER TWO
When to Retreat.

At one time Purah had been a stout woman. She was slowly succumbing to a failing body riddled with arthritis and osteoporosis but always looking for a new adventure.

Buckling her seatbelt, "Gid, we've got a few minutes. We haven't driven out in the country lately. Why don't we just take the long way to church?"

"Baby, I am thinking the same thing."

As they drove past the grove in Harbor Oaks River Park, Gid asked, "Why do you think they have whitewashed those oak trees?"

"It is a nice touch. It looks so fresh and clean. It seems to give dimension to the park. It is as though things are more noticeable. I wonder if it was done to add an old-fashioned charm for us 'old folks' to enjoy, you know, to cause us to reminisce? Nowadays, it may be for looks, but in our day, whitewashing served a purpose."

Crazy Granny's House

Fixing his eyes on the grove beside the river where the Lord appeared to him, then slowing the car, "It was right there, Purah. This *Closing Life's Challenge* must be monumental. My mind won't let it go."

"Will it be evangelistic, Gid?"

"I know it will involve you. We are one flesh." Chuckling, "You learned to read my thoughts a long time ago. I know how you will react in certain situations."

The rain had subsided, and everything had a soft green glow as though God had just given new life with a good scrubbing. Purah took a deep breath, commenting, "Nothing smells better."

"Gid said, "I know with this extra humidity, it will make my breathing even more labored.

"You remember, here at the confluence of the rivers, we spent so much time during our childhood. Miller's folks' mill was just over the next ridge. Our family ferry was on over at Mosquito Fjord."

"I remember, Gid. Let's drive over to Ochre's place. He told me he just couldn't change a thing, even after all these years. Everything is showing such disrepair, though."

"There is his grandmother's little shack where his mother died. That shack may be his only memory of his mother," said Gid.

Purah said, "Look, Gid, Ochre is out there now."

Gid said, "Let's see if we can inch down into Fish Milk Holler. It won't be easy. The path is eroded and some of the saplings are bent over, into the yard."

Gid cut the engine.

"Hold my hand while I walk on this spongy ground, Gid. This may have been a bad idea. We need to go through the brush and around the gravestones to get up on the porch. This place is creepy, Gid."

"What is that awful sound? Creature or bird? Someone is wailing, Gid!"

The door stood open.

Gid, stepping onto the porch, yelled. "'When the border of the Hague and the coast requite, it's time to retreat.'"

Silence, then you could hear Ochre laughing like a hyena. "Come in here, you buzzard. Oh, I haven't heard that in a month of Sundays."

"It is fascinating, Gid, how a little humor breaks a tense moment," commented Purah while she entered an open-spaced room with fireplace, a cradle, a wash bowl, a catch-all, and an eating table and chair.

Ochre, one of their crew from childhood, was still in the grips of his painful past. Educating himself as a social worker was his feeble attempt to understand and organize his premature thoughts and memories of his mother's untimely tragic death. His baggage seemed to continue piling up. Gid tried tirelessly to understand Ochre's jealous spirit and haughty yet cunning attitude. Now, aging and health issues developed into incapacities for Ochre.

Ochre's small brim fedora always had a half smoked cigarette in the band. The crew all joked about it, but he said he kept it there for emergencies.

"Ochre, we were out for a little ride before church, and saw you here," said Gid, noting the dry, curled timbers of the table. "This place holds a lot of memories for you, Ochre."

Taking a slow breath and trying to regain his composure, Ocher responded, "I have a fragmented dream at times that I can't help but wonder the meaning."

Ochre's lifestyle had many failed attempts at coping with his past. He was gripping both sides of the ladderback chair, while trying to break his sobs. "Gid, how do you know when it is time to cut and run?" Breathing deeply, "I can barely even say it, but to sell this place?

"In the dream, I am dropping a small, heavy bucket into a hole. You both know, I stop by occasionally. I feel a closeness to my mother here. She died slumped over this table. She had been eating her soup while Daddy's cousin Gladys had gone to the neighbors to borrow cornmeal for supper. My baby brother was there in the cradle beside the hearth, when we found Mama. My 'Crazy Granny' was wandering around in here, just picking up everything and putting it back down. She couldn't even talk anymore.

"Cousin Gladys said, 'Crazy Granny probably gave her something to eat that killed her.'"

"So, is that what you always believed?" Gid asked. "What was listed as her cause of death?"

"I do remember when the doctor came. He said something about possible sepsis, from the birth. I suppose in those days, adults didn't talk to kids about those things."

Gid asked, "What do you remember about your cousin Gladys?"

"I remember how she smelled. She always smelled like smoke and snuff. That cheap dime store perfume mixed with that smell was sickening. She had tight flat curls around her face and wore rouge and red lipstick.

"She came to help Mama 'cause the baby was coming. Cousin Gladys soon went back home."

Purah said, "I remember her. Oh yes, I remember how she would come to our house selling eggs. She would just walk in and prop her foot on Mama's chair, like she owned the place. She wasn't a pleasant person. Every time I saw her, she dissed me about my hair. She let me know I was not acceptable to her. Comments like, 'What did you do to your hair,' or 'did your sister do your hair today?'"

"You always remember how a person makes you feel, said Purah. "Now, as an adult I know she had a heart problem, but as a child she was giving *me* a heart problem."

"Purah," said Gid, "it is amazing that you remember her. You were so young."

Gid, commenting, "So, as an adult, you never looked into her death, Ochre?"

Lost in time, after all those years, Ochre labored to answer. "After Daddy died, we found her death certificate said, 'Death consistent with poison.'"

"Ochre, do you believe your Granny was able to rationalize enough to carry out a thought, a plan?"

"You know, Gid, I have never thought of it that way. She came to live with us after that and she was total care. She couldn't even verbalize a sentence. Her speech was garbled and agitated. She could not follow instructions. She couldn't feed herself when you put the food in her hand. She didn't live long after that. There was a lot we didn't know about dementia in those days."

Ocher continued, "Looking back, I believe she died of dehydration. But, to answer your question, she couldn't follow your instructions, much less make a plan."

"I really wonder if more was known about your mother's death than you ever knew, Ochre?"

Gid had never been one to give up on anything easily. His tenacious spirit helped him minister in many difficult situations. "Ochre, you have got to find peace in all this!"

It was becoming obvious, Gid was giving out of breath and could not stand much longer. "Ochre, why don't you check *The Lighthouse News and Views* archives for anything in the paper? Your mother's death by poison would have been big news in this little community."

As they walked out the door, "You are so right, Gid, why haven't I thought of that? I have been absorbed with immature emotion for all these years. My brain just shut down when it came to assimilating all of this. I will get on this first thing in the morning."

"Ochre, you can be objective about it now," said Gid. "Don't leave any stone unturned."

#

"Purah! Don't go in church yet, said Gid."

With each word, his voice began to trail off. "Purah, we haven't had a chance to talk about my...my diagnosis and what Dr. Lucas told me today."

"Gid, I knew you would tell me when you are ready."

"Baby, I always thought I would be ready...for the end."

Reaching for his hand, weeping, "Dear Lord, please, no. Oh, Gid, are you?

"Dying?"

Gid, gaining his composure, "I need more time."

"What are you saying?"

"There isn't anything more they can do, Purah."

Through her tears, "There is no new medicine to try?"

"He is ordering Hospice.

"I don't know how I made it home from the Park today. We laughed about Miller praying like a wild man.

"It had to be my guardian angel. My feet felt so heavy, I was shuffling with each step. I was laboring to breathe.

"Purah, they order Hospice when you are in the end stage of your disease."

"Gid, this is too much for you. Our service starts in moments. Let's sit here quietly and regain our composure."

Gid said, "They are ringing the Charity Grace bell. Let's go on in."

CHAPTER THREE
The Exhortation

(Setting: The Zion Chapel at Harbor Oaks Assisted Living)

The picturesque sanctuary lacked nothing in efficiency for worship. The choir loft had amazing acoustics—no need for a sound system. Pews were comfortably upholstered, with kneeling benches in front of each. There was an air of antiquity, yet all state-of-the-art accoutrements, from the pulpit furniture to the ornate bell and headstock, taken from an old ship, used to toll *The Charity Grace*. Its current use was tolling the beginning of all services, from the Sunday morning worship to the marriages, births, baptisms, and deaths.

Beginning to be seated, neighbors were interacting as Maude shared the disastrous afternoon of Reverend Gideon being caught in the storm.

They all loved Gid so much and were fighting the grief of his congestive heart failure. Loving Gid was easy. He lived his life finding ways to help his neighbor.

"We were all worried sick and were about to report back to Purah that we couldn't find him, when, in he walked," Maude said. "Each of us was drenched from the driving rain, and there he stood completely dry. I am here to tell you, not even a raindrop on him."

"Maude," whispered Miller, "maybe the Lord would want us to ponder on this some more. It deserves our attention and may give us a new insight. I believe God is about to map out a new itinerary for us here at Harbor Oaks Assisted Living."

"There is something in the Bible about a dry fleece," he said.

The choir sang their rendition of "Way Maker,"[6] with the orchestra strings reverberating in close legato harmony, along with a lyrical countermelody, creating a descant for the choir.

David Adams, music minister's, long bowing technique on the double bass caused the worshippers to feel a deep vibrato in their chest. The texture alone of that bass/baritone foundation served glory to the creator.

David, with his attention to every detail of his orderly dress, down to the freshly cut boutonniere, was deeply consumed with the presentation of delicate phrasing within the piece.

With the upbeat, David gently drew the words of 'Way Maker' from the choir as though he were slowly drawing in a rope.

The Exhortation
Like a Tree

With humble distinction, Reverend Gideon methodically assumed his position in the pulpit. Placing his hands on the pulpit, with his face turned upward in prayer, after a brief pause, he said, "I am just glad to be in the house. Holy Spirit, I am glad *You* are in the house.

With half-cocked face, as though looking through one eye, "Precious friends, today, our reader will be reading from Jeremiah 17:5-9. Blessed be the reading of The Word.

"Let us stand in reverence and in awe."

---

[6] (Sinach 2015)

Cursed be the man that trusteth in man, and maketh flesh his arm, and whose heart departeth from the Lord.

For he shall be like the heath in the desert, and shall not see when good cometh; but shall inhabit the parched places in the wilderness, in a salt land and not inhabited.

Blessed is the man that trusteth in the Lord, and whose hope the Lord is.

For he shall be as a tree planted by the waters, and that spreadeth out her roots by the river, and shall not see when heat cometh, but her leaf shall be green; and shall not be careful in the year of drought, neither shall cease from yielding fruit.

The heart is deceitful above all things, and desperately wicked: who can know it? Jer 17:5-9[7]

Holding tightly to the horns of the pulpit, Reverend Gideon began.

"Like a Tree."

"You elders *are* the trees." Taking a short breath, "Yes, you, and you, mamas and papas, and the boys and the girls. Yes, all God's children."

Hearing the scripture, Ochre could only focus on "Cursed be the man that trusteth in man, and maketh flesh his arm, and whose heart departeth from the Lord" Jer. 17:5.[8]

Reverend Gideon waited as he heard, "Yes, amen, well."

"You will be extending your lifeline of your root system into the stream of the spirit of God," he said.

"Preach it!" The congregation was energetically engaged by now.

---

[7] ((KJV) n.d.)
[8] ((KJV) n.d.)

Ochre could hardly concentrate. *"The heart is deceitful above all things, and desperately wicked: who can know it?" Jer 17:9.*[9] Now, focusing, *"heart," "deceitful," "desperate," "wicked!"*

Gid continued, "Extending your lifeline into the lifegiving fountain. You are stepping out into that cool clear water. Brothers and sisters, your lifeline is your anchor!"

"Amens" were coming from all over the room.

"Yes, yes," said Dr. Morrison.

Reverend Gideon continued. "The heat, I said the heat can't wilt your passion." Pausing to catch his breath, "It can't scorch you because, I said, the heat can't scorch you because you have no fear. Fear comes from the enemy. You all know our enemy well. That old slew-foot. He is a liar. Yes, he turns up the heat of our circumstances and wilts our passion."

With that, the worshippers stood and clapped and cheered. "You know it, Brother Gid!"

"Preach it, Pastor."

"Aaamen."

"You have demonstrated the newness of life in righteousness. You have led others into that new life with freshness, and purity and fruitfulness. Yes, I said 'fruitfulness.' We will prosper despite circumstances. The circumstances of the drought of our aging bodies, the drought of our handicaps, the drought of loss of homes, the drought of loss of our ambulation, drought of loss of loved ones.

"But does our life consist of outward things?

With a victory shout he began—

---

[9] (Ibid n.d.)

"We

"Will

"Yet

"Bear

"Fruit!

"Our last season is not passed. Our last season will be our most fruitful. Our fruit will bear fruit, and that fruit will bear more fruit. Friends, our last season just began. Reader, please read Psalm 1:3...."

And he shall be like a tree planted by the rivers of water, that bringeth forth his fruit in his season; his leaf also shall not wither; and whatsoever he doeth shall prosper.[10]

Looking around the room, "Each of you are trees, you are mighty *Oaks*, that are rooted in love and nurtured by God's Grace," then pausing for the amens.

"Beloved, we fight our battles on our knees. Is there anything that our God can't do?"

Miller stood, as though bearing a battle flag. "Nothing is too hard for God," while waving his frail bent arm from side to side.

Gid emphatically quoted JER 32:17. "'Ah Lord God! behold, thou hast made the heaven and the earth by thy great power and stretched out arm, and there is nothing too hard for thee:'"[11]

After a pause, "My friends," making eye contact with different individuals around the room, "God impressed on my heart, we will engage in another battle. What that will be is yet unknown.

---

[10] ((KJV) n.d.)
[11] ((KJV) n.d.)

"We will know it when it comes. Allow me to encourage you." Pausing, "That battle, my friends, is our Alpha Omega God's. Yes, He knows the end from the beginning. He knows our uprising and our down sittings. He numbered the very hairs of our heads."

Pausing, "He knew our days before there was one of them. Our job, I said, our job is to be patient.

"Our bodies are not strong. We will exchange our strength for his, our weapons for his, our garments for his. He will give us the battle plan" (Ref. 1 Sam 18:4).[12]

The Oaks all stood waving their frail hands and swaying, while holding the pews.

Reverend Gideon stated emphatically, "I feel the unity. I feel cooperation. We will yield fruit in season. My friends, Our God will provide. Yes, Our God will provide!"

"We will enter a season of waiting. Oaks, please, be in an attitude of prayer."

As Gid was stepping down from the pulpit, his personal attendant Rose assisted him into the wheelchair. Gid's day was completed, and he was consumed.

Rose Taylor, tall and stout, had been the Gideons' personal attendant since they moved to Assisted Living. Chores were always completed with promptness, giving little time for casual conversation. Rose was always interested, though, in spiritual talk and sometimes asked questions.

Preaching for Gid was now so laborious. The fluid he was retaining and collecting around his heart was causing the shortness of breath that so characterized his illness and disabled his once energetic body. "Let's head home, Rose."

---

[12] ((KJV) n.d.)

Rose was visibly moved by the service that night.

"Reverend Gid, you have done used up yourself." Stooping over, she put his feet in the supports and began to wheel him home.

They passed Ochre, who gritted his teeth and whispered to Rose. Gid heard him say, "Give it up, Rose!"

Gid noticed that Rose was visibly disturbed but didn't comment.

"Yes, Rose," said Gid, "that is how the Lord works. The apostle Paul said in 2 Cor 12:10, 'for when I am weak, then am I strong.'[13]

"I am broken. I had about three more points in that scripture, but just spent myself.

"That scripture in Psalms 1:1 says: 'Blessed is the man that walketh not in the counsel of the ungodly, nor standeth in the way of sinners, nor sitteth in the seat of the scornful.'[14]

"I *am* a blessed man, even though broken physically, but I have more to give than ever."

Gid was struggling to get the next breath. He believed Rose needed to hear this.

"All our Oaks have prayed about being able to leave a legacy." He took a slow shallow breath. "Now we have physical limitations." Closing his eyes, with labored breathing, "We couldn't imagine helping even one person."

"Mr. Gid, you need to get some rest."

"Rose, that is when God uses you the most. He takes our weaknesses (pause) and magnifies His glory. In my weakness, he is giving me my *Closing Life-Challenge*."

---

[13] ((KJV) n.d.)
[14] ((KJV) n.d.)

"Mr. Gid, you prop those feet up when you get in the bed. They look like water balloons."

"Thank you, Rose, you always know just what to do. I will see you in the morning."

"Purah, see if you can help steady me. I should have let Rose help me into bed."

"Gid you just sit on the side of the bed, and I will help you swing your feet up." Stepping back, "Oh, Jesus, help us."

"What?"

"Gid, your legs are weeping. Fluid is running down both of your legs into your shoes. I will call your Hospice nurse; this is an emergency."

#

"Connie, thank you for hurrying."

"Ms. Purah, when I am on call, I stay ready to go out. Bring me his supplies, please."

"Mr. Gid, I am going to wrap your legs in gauze. We sure don't want them to get infected.

"How much diuretic have you taken today?"

"Just regular, then I took the PRN dose as soon as I got home from prayer meeting."

"If you lie down with this much fluid, it will fill your lungs," Connie said. "Try sleeping in your recliner tonight. I'll be right back—I left something in the car."

Purah was standing at his head. Gid reached for her hand. "Baby, this must have been serious."

Connie was back in a flash. "I just had to make my report to Dr. Solomon. Taking a chair over to face him, "I am going to stay the night. I need to monitor your breathing."

"Connie, will I make it through this?"

"Reverend Gideon, it could go either way. That is why I am staying. You remember before, you would end up in the ER. With Hospice, you won't be going back to the hospital."

"So, I will die at home?"

"Yes, Reverend Gideon. You will be able to be in the comfort of your home, with your loved ones."

"Baby, call the Oaks."

"Reverend Gideon, there could be many of these episodes. Let's wait a few minutes."

Putting her arm around Purah, Connie said, "Just get me a blanket. I will rest here beside his chair. You can sleep there on the sofa if you wish."

It was a sleepless night for the threesome. The diuretic did its job. Gid struggled to the bedside potty numerous times.

Into the night, Gid's respirations improved. "Mrs. Gideon, it looks like he made a turnaround—this time. Taking that PRN dose of diuretic may have made the difference."

"Oh, thank you, dear Jesus," said Purah.

Squeezing Purah's hand, Gid said, "Thank you for the prayers, baby."

35

CHAPTER FOUR
Season of Waiting.

Next morning came with Rose wheeling Gid back from the restroom. "Let me catch my breath," said Rose. "Mr. Gid, I just can't get these wheels locked."

As Rose transferred Gid to his recliner, he observed how quiet and distraught she seemed. "Rose, is there something I can help you with? You are not yourself."

Slowly inhaling, with tears streaming, "I don't want to trouble you, Reverend. I know you have your own concerns. My tenth child will be coming before long, and I am at wits' end with decisions."

Purah reached for her hand.

"Ya see, my husband is an ineffective alcoholic." Rose began to wring the towel in her hand. "He can't keep a job; we have bills to pay. We have seven children in school and two still at home."

Wiping tears with the towel, "Reverend, my husband doesn't know about this child. I have been able to hide my pregnancy. I done already gained a lot of weight."

Rose couldn't hold back the tears. "I feel I need to give it up for adoption." Sobbing, "That would be the best thing for the baby and for my other children."

Trying to regain her composure, "This rips a mother's heart out. More than anything, I need your prayers." Almost wailing, "Reverend, I love this child, more than you know."

"Rose, may I share this with the Oaks? You know we believe in the power of prayer."

"Yes, sir, Mr. Gid, I need help from the Almighty."

"Rose, you do need to tell your husband. It is his right to know."

Rose left Harbor Oaks that day with a heavy heart. She was in labor.

The next day, Rose did not show up for work. Maude learned from Nathaniel the Chef, that Rose had been sick on Thursday.

#

As usual, the Oaks met at the Gideons' apartment for morning coffee.

Miller didn't just pray; he was in the scripture daily. He said, "The Lord brought me to his scripture, y'all. This is about the dry fleece. The 'dry fleece' (Ju 6:36)[15] was a sign.

"I believe the Lord is going to use our Gideon to fight a mighty battle. In the Bible, God used Gideon to lead a weak group of people to fight a major battle. They were outnumbered, '450:1,'[16] and won the battle through the almighty power of God. They knew that it was God's will that they fight this battle, but only God could give them the victory. Y'all, this battle God is leading us to fight—we will win.

"It is His will; it is His battle. We are weak warriors.

---

[15] ((KJV) n.d.)
[16] (Shirer 2013, 2019)

"We are dry, thirsty fleeces. We have all prayed for God to use our knowledge and experiences, even though we are old, sick, thirsty, frail, handicapped, and beyond fruitfulness. I don't know what the odds will be, but it is God's battle, it is His victory."

"That is good encouragement," said Purah.

#

Friday morning routine brought Rose along with her housekeeping cart into Gid and Purah's apartment.

Ochre's arrival was delayed after his morning skydive. Slipping into the apartment, it seemed like an eternity before he found his usual seat in the old rocking chair. Scruffy looked at Ochre and said, "You know that is my seat."

Now Scruffy was Miller's dog, but Ochre took to spoiling him every morning at coffee time.

Ochre scooped Scruffy up and began whispering into his ear. Scruffy climbed up on Ochre's chair back and laid his head on Ochre's shoulder.

David's big ear was always tuned in. "What did he say, Ochre?"

"David, Scruffy said, 'where is my ice cream?'"

"Yep, sounds like you have him spoiled."

Rose's demeanor was peculiar. She did not notice the entire clan was in the parlor, including Scruffy. Rose proceeded with the dreariness of her routine, making their beds, and assisting with Purah's and Gid's baths. Oddly, she would disappear with Scruffy following her every step. Then she would quickly reappear.

As she came into the parlor, Gid asked if they could pray with her. "Rose, our hearts are heavy for you. I shared your need with our Oaks." She slipped to her knees and began wiping tears with her apron.

The room was thick with God's glory. You could smell the prayers as though they were incense being burned as an offering. The faces of each of the Oaks seemed to glow with a clear holiness. Dr. and Mrs. Morrison were holding Gid's hands up as he was praying for Rose and her baby.

In the quietness of the room, Miller began to sing his prayer in short sentences. The Oaks were actively involved in antiphonal response. "Oh, Lord, give her wisdom…!"

Response: "Oh Lord, give her wisdom…!"

"That it would be a garland of Grace on her head."

Response: "That it would be a garland of Grace on her head" (Prov. 4:9).[17]

Then, there fell a silence in that room for an untold amount of time.

Momentarily, they heard the church bell tolling. The Charity Grace was tolling, and then: a baby's cry.

Intense reality was in the room.

Rose stepped forward. "This is what I need you to do for me, Reverend and Mrs. Gideon. I need you to watch her tonight. I brought her formula and diapers. I need tonight to work something out.

"God will direct you. Let me finish up and go. There is so much to be done." Rose calmly said, "Call her Charity Grace."

Purah's eyes met Gid's.

[17] Scripture taken from the NEW AMERICAN STANDARD BIBLE®, Copyright © 1960, 1962, 1963, 1968, 1971, 1972, 1973, 1975, 1977, 1995 by The Lockman Foundation. Used by permission.

With quiet resolve, Rose left the room, finished cleaning the bathroom, and slipped out.

"Call her Charity Grace," they each repeated.

No one knew that Rose had slipped a note between the bath towels, not to be found until later.

#

Clearing his throat, Gid attempts to stand. "Oaks, before you go, I guess there is never a good time for bad news. With all the business, I have not given you my doctor report."

Labored breathing. "Dr. Lucas ordered Hospice for me."

Gid began to weep. The Oaks had rarely seen him in a weak moment.

"That usually means you are not expected to live more than six months," cried Purah.

Miller said, "Gid, we have already been praying for you. Things are getting clearer as we go along. We are not ignoring this, but we are not receiving this. I just don't believe it is time."

"Miller, my spirit is troubled. I feel I still have so much to do.

"You all should know; I had a close call night before last."

Dr. Morrison said, "Gid, just keep doing what you have always done. Take your time."

"Time, I don't have. This *Closing Life-Challenge*, I do have, in God's timing."

CHAPTER FIVE
Rose Taylor's absence

"Purah, I know I have told you this story before, but just indulge me."

Gid had begun to reminisce frequently since his diagnosis.

"My brother, Manly and I would walk to and from school. I was just a little second-grader who came home *alone* one day to an empty house.

"In desperation, I called, 'Mama, Daddy, Manly, where are you?'

"I ran from room to room, and everything was gone. My folk had moved off and left me. Sharecroppers moved frequently from farm to farm to find work, in those days.

"Hungry and thirsty, my little heart almost exploded as I sat on those old wooden steps and cried into my dirty hands. I had never had to solve any of life's problems and didn't know where to begin.

"Neighbors would pass and throw up their hands. They didn't know.

"I just sat there and cried. The more I cried, the more scared I got.

"Just before dark, my brother Manly came walking up and said, 'Come on, boy, let's go home.' He acted like nothing.

"My chest was pounding and by that time I was snubbing. My whole life had just ended.

"I learned when we got home that he was supposed to have met me as soon as I got to the house.

Manly and I were never close after that. He had always intimidated me. Now that barrier was planted.

"That day in my life traumatized me for years, but it is the one thing that led me to the Lord. When I learned he would never forsake me, I knew that is what I needed—not just wanted. His Spirit's presence is my comfort, all these years. Purah, he never leaves me."

#

Gid sat rocking little Charity Grace, admiring her perfect hands, fingernails, the tiny nose, while Purah answered emails from some of her former students. Gid was just talking away, "Having a child around is not out of the ordinary for us."

They never had children of their own yet had mentored countless individuals over the past sixty years of marriage, with Purah having taught speech and communication courses at the local university. Their home was a bustling haven for young student teachers and pastors who were soaking up the wisdom of this loving couple.

"Purah," said Gid, "nurturing those college students was nothing like having this sweet little darling snuggling against my neck, with her tiny little body rolled up like a soft ball."

#

The Oaks gathered at Reverend Gideon's apartment, with Mrs. Morrison leading the inquiry. "Gid, we need to take account of this situation while continuing prayer for Rose and her husband. Just what do we know about Rose's husband?

1. He fathered ten children.
2. He is an ineffective alcoholic.

3. He seldom works.
4. He does not know about Charity Grace.

"What we do *not* know about him:

1. His name
2. Where he lives
3. How old he is.
4. How to get in touch with him

"This is Sunday and we have not heard from Rose, Gid. She surely needed some recuperation time. I wonder if she will try to work tomorrow. Maybe, we can watch Charity Grace some for her. She is such a pleasant child."

#

Ochre checked in with the Gideons. "This is Tuesday and we still have not heard from Rose. I think I will go by the office and ask about her. This will give me a chance to try out my new scooter."

Ochre knocked on the administrator, Suzanne's door. "May I come in?"

"Sure, Ochre, come on in. Make yourself at home. Can I get you something? Maybe some water?"

"Water would be good, thank you."

Ochre walked with a stiffness visible even in his neck and shoulders. "Let me take a seat in this straight chair beside your desk, Suzanne. Straight chairs seem to be easier to get out of these days."

"Ochre, I just have to ask you something, maybe it is not too personal."

"Certainly. Ask away."

"I have been puzzled by you and your friends. I have never witnessed anything like it. You all act like family. Your responsibility and concern toward one another are that of brothers and sisters, or maybe even like parent and child."

Ochre began to consider that himself. "I think back to our school days. We were all in school together. It was extremely hard times for all our parents."

"I know you have a lot of Great Depression stories," said Suzanne. "Those stories make me reflect on my own life. I wonder if I have the grit it would take to carry me through that kind of adversity."

Struggling to get comfortable, leaning to one side, Ochre said, "Just like everywhere else, a large majority of people in this town had lost their jobs. No one had money. It would not matter if we did; there were no goods to buy."

"So, you remember those hard times?"

"Oh, yes. Our clothes were made from flour sacks, we all had gardens, we would hunt and fish for food, we borrowed tools, bartered with our produce and eggs. You won't believe this, but people didn't have clothes closets. We could hang everything we owned on a nail on the back of a door.

"Why, we had neighbor children that would steal from our coal pile."

"Coal? Whatever for?"

"Ms. Suzanne, I guess they were cold. They never got much at a time. We would hear them at night. Daddy said to leave them alone.

"They would even steal from people's gardens.

"I remember seeing Dr. Owens wash his car in the creek. Even he couldn't buy tires—there weren't any.

"I believe more than anything, we survived because we loved one another and shared one another's burdens.

"We had a teacher, Everette Weeks, who poured himself into us boys and girls. He said, 'Now you boys and girls have a lot to learn, and I have a lot to teach.' He demonstrated every day how he loved us and taught us the golden rule. His friendship was for everyone." A little teary-eyed, "He always grinned at us with those snuff-stained teeth."

"I'm sorry, Suzanne, I could go on and on."

"Ochre, please. These stories are invaluable. They are what our country is based on, don't you think? Perseverance and grit are noble character traits. Tell me more, please."

"My own family became dysfunctional through the years, with my two older sisters being killed in a train accident.

"That teacher took a special interest in me. I really cannot imagine where I would be today if he had not helped me through that. My father was so overcome with grief that he would not even speak their names. I was too young to understand death and separation."

"You didn't have anybody?" asked Suzanne.

"You have heard of hard knocks? I lived it, Suzanne."

"My only consolation—don't know if it were a dream or if it were real, but Jesus would come and hold me when I would cry.

"I remember He had a beard and was strong, but *my* Jesus had short hair. Hehehe. That is the only love shown me, until Mr. and Mrs. Weeks came."

"Did Jesus continue to come after Mr. Weeks came?"

"Not in person, but I knew he was there."

Playground fun with beloved teacher

"Before the accident, my sisters both loved me and played with me like I was their own baby. They spent time helping me with homework, doing chores, and singing at night. We had already lost our mother. Because of the way Daddy worked, all my brother and I had was our sisters."

"I remember the time we milked that cow and poured it on our dog from the barn loft. Rex liked it. He licked himself down good, but Daddy could never figure out why he smelled so rank. Every time Daddy mentioned how bad Rex smelled, we laughed until we wet our pants. Those are the days that were lost after the accident."

"I am so sorry to hear about the train accident, Ochre. Did your dad ever remarry, after your mother's death?"

With a huff, "Yeah but that is a story for another day. Things didn't go well. She had three sons of her own, and my dad never really managed emotionally after my mom's death. He was abusive to her boys."

"So, you have had a sad childhood, but you have had a very successful career."

"My career is a result of the tragedy I suffered as a child. It colors every decision throughout my life, Suzanne. I have been a scoundrel. Binge drinking doesn't help matters any. My life is filled with swirls of garbage, deposited in the drift."

"Was Purah in your class?"

Ochre responded, "Why? Yes, yes, she was," "We have known each other most all of our lives."

"Oh, Ochre, sorry to interrupt. I want you to listen to Purah, out in the foyer," she said.

"Ochre, do you know she comes over every day and stands out there in the foyer, welcoming everyone who enters this building. You would think she is our hostess. She hugs them all. She hugs residents, the family members, the postman, the foodservice salesman, and the ambulance drivers. She always ends her receptions with a poem about hugs.

Suzanne shakes her pointed finger to direct Ochre's attention. "Listen, she is out there now."

"Ah, ah, ah," said Purah in a shrill voice. "We are so glad to see you today," as the occupational therapist came in carrying her therapy bag. "We just want you to know we love you and appreciate all you do for us. We want you to know how much we care about you. You know that 'people don't care how much you know, until they know how much you care,'"[18] she said.

"Yes, Purah was a college professor," said Ochre. "That love of hers was like honey dripping on those students. She never fails to make a person feel loved and appreciated. She was able to stimulate their learning in gifted ways. She still offers so much. Ms. Suzanne, Purah Gideon is for real.

"Gid is nobody's fool. He knew right away she was a keeper."

"Oh, Ochre, you came over here for a reason. What can I do for you? I hope there isn't a problem."

Nervously, "Our group noticed Rose's absence. We are concerned about Rose. We haven't seen her since Friday. Is she okay, Suzanne?"

"Rose? Let me see what I can find out. I do know her supervisor has not heard from her. Nowadays, people will do a no-call, no-show without much thought. Rose doesn't have a telephone. I will let you know what we can find out," she said.

"Oh, here comes Nat, said Ochre. He'll know. Excuse me, Ms. Suzanne."

"Hey, Nat, what's up?"

---

[18] (Roosevelt, No known source n.d.)

Nathaniel had that all-knowing grin on his face but didn't comment. "Ochre, are you up to sumpin'?"

"Just on a fact-finding mission. You are the one I should ask, Nat. You always know everything that is going on around here. When do you ever have time to cook?"

"Okay, maybe I do know jes about everthin'."

Nathaniel knew what Ochre wanted. Dodging the confrontation, he said, "You and David be heppin' me tomorrow? That's gonna be a lotta work."

"Nat, you are changing the subject."

"Just leeme see what I can do, Ochre."

Nathaniel was always careful not to divulge too much information. You would never find him revealing his sources.

Ochre, gritting his teeth with every word, "Nat, have you talked to Rose?"

"Rose be bad sick, Ochre."

"What else do you know, Nat?"

"Here's your menu."

"Be my friend, Nat."

"It's not my place, Ochre. You be knowin' soon enuf."

As Ochre turned to leave, Purah walked into the dining room. "This burden is too heavy for you to carry, Ochre."

Looking through her, he was wondering: Just what did she mean? Does Purah know?

#

Calling law enforcement, Suzanne asked them to do a wellness check on Rose.

51

Early the next morning, the local deputy came to the residence office. "Mrs. Suzanne Josephson, I am the Harbor Oaks constable. It is my duty to give you the sad news that Rose Taylor passed away."

"Oh, that can't be, Constable."

"Mrs. Josephson, little is known at this time about the details. Her husband will need to be your contact for additional information. Good day, Madam."

Suzanne determined a personal visit to Ochre's apartment was best to convey this message. "Oh, Ochre, I am so sorry to bring you such heartbreaking news. Our sweet Rose has died."

"Uh, uh, what happened?"

"The Constable told me; Rose's husband didn't know of anything wrong with her. He did know she had not felt well. I will let you know when I hear the arrangements."

"This is such a shock, Suzanne. I need time to wrap my mind around this."

Ochre had been a social worker much of his career and had been appointed to the position of director of the State Department of Family Services. Ochre thought, *Rose's death would create a complicated situation for the Oaks, where Charity Grace was concerned.*

"I wonder if this is anything to do with the Reverend's teaching, on Wednesday evening—" he said under his breath. "Could this be our 'Closing Life-Challenge?'"

CHAPTER SIX
Ambition: Make a Friend Every Day

Over at the nursing home next door, Gid was closing the day's devotion. "Miller will accompany us on the guitar, singing, 'All Hail the Power of Jesus Name.'"[19]

Nobody knew how Miller could still play that guitar with a crooked arm and arthritic fingers.

"Reverend Gideon, I sure enjoyed your visit today," said little Ethel.

Ethel sat there in her wheelchair, guarding the elevator wearing her fluffy pink gloves, in the middle of summer, simply happy as you please.

"Ethel, tell me again about your ambition in life," said Miller.

Without hesitation, "My ambition in life is to try to make a friend every day. You know God loves people and we're supposed to love everybody."

"Did your mother teach you that?" he said.

---

[19] (Perrronet 1779)

With joy in her heart and a smile on her face, "Sure. I was raised by the Golden Rule: 'Do unto others as you would have them do unto you.'"

Miller said, "Miss Ethel, do you mind if we pray for you?"

"I need your prayer," she said. "I pray for y'all every day."

Miller, feeble as he was, slipped down to kneel beside her wheelchair.

As he reached for her hand, Ethel started talking to God like he was just one of their group. "Lord, I hope you are being good to these boys. They are so good to me. They visit me every week. Thank you, Jesus."

Miller began to intercede for her. "Oh, Lord, you know Miss Ethel is such a blessing to us. Her stories just feed our hungry souls.

"Lord, I thank you that she is able to remember the words and sing harmony for us as we worship.

"We ask that you fill her lonely hours with sweet memories and give her opportunities to minister your love to those who provide her care.

"Lord, when it comes Miss Ethel's time to cross over, may the ones who are witnesses smell that sweet aroma of the incense of her prayers for them. In the name above every name, Jesus!"

"You know, Gid, these people are still giving of themselves. They are just who they are."

"Let's head home, Miller. Purah will be home soon."

#

Miller said, "Let's go by Gordon Pollard's room and pray with him before we go."

"Gordon Pollard? Is he any kin to Snitch Pollard?"

"Yeah. That's him. I heard he is pretty low," said Miller.

#

Purah had hoped to make a quick trip to the Baby Mart to pick up needed items. She was rushing out to the car and stepped off the walk onto an uneven pavement. Purah, with mournful cries, "Why was I in such a hurry? Ohh!"

The ambulance arrived in minutes, but it seemed like days.

"Ma'am, can you move your legs? Did you hit your head?"

"Oh, I don't know. Oh, my back!"

"We are putting a neck brace on you and slipping this board under you. Try to breathe deep and slow. We will be restraining you, ma'am, for your safety." Releasing the latch on the gurney, "easy up, Mam."

#

Gid got home and relieved Maude from her sitting duties. He reached to answer the phone while rocking Charity Grace.

"Reverend Gideon, this is Mildred, the ER nurse. Your wife took a nasty fall at the Baby Mart. She is in x-ray now. She will want to see you as soon as she is out."

Easing out of the chair, Gid put Charity Grace in the cradle. Grabbing the phone again, "Pansie, I need backup. Purah is in ER being x-rayed after a fall in town."

"Be right there," Gid.

Another phone call. "Miller, can you and Maude go with me to the ER? I do not know what I am facing. Purah fell."

"Sure thing, buddy, be right over."

Miller began to wail, "Oh God, give the doctors wisdom. Purah needs a miracle."

Maude said, "Here, let me drive to the ER, Gid. You and Miller aren't in any shape."

Letting them out at the door, "I'll park the car and be right in."

#

"Reverend Gideon, from the x-rays, your wife shows numerous compression fractures, from the past. This time, she fractured the L2 and L3. She is heavily sedated now, but you can go in to see her."

"Baby, what happened?"

Purah smiled but was reaching for objects in the air. He knew he would not get answers until the sedation wore off.

Grasping her hand, "I'll be right here, Baby."

Looking around the room, he noticed some grocery bags.

"Miller, what is in those bags?"

"Baby formula."

"Uh-huh. She had gone out to buy supplies for the baby." With a little chuckle, "I guess the EMT driver delivered the formula too."

Gid, looking heavenward, rubbing the tension from his weathered face, "Dear God, are we too old for this?"

#

"Nurse, when will the doctor be around?"

"He makes his rounds at 8 a.m."

"Reverend Gideon."

"Dr. Lucas, I am so glad you are her attending physician."

"Gid, compression fractures are very painful. You can be extremely thankful she didn't break a hip too.

"The discharge planner is making her a follow-up appointment with Dr. Moss, the orthopedic doctor, tomorrow. He will do the procedure this morning. She needs bed rest for a couple of days. They have made great strides in treatment for this type of fracture if she is a candidate."

#

Meeting the physician outside her door, "Dr. Moss, have you taken her back?"

"Reverend Gideon, the procedure is complete. We injected the glue in two vertebrae. This is an extraordinarily successful procedure. She will feel immediate relief. For those who are candidates, it gives them back their mobility, virtually pain-free."

Surprised, "Doc, I don't know how to thank you. Our lives are planned out for a long time to come."

"Allow her to rest a couple of days, and she will be as good as new," said Dr. Moss.

#

Purah's pain in her spine had been enhanced with the newly collapsed vertebrae. The relief was a welcome friend.

Once she was home, the Oaks, one by one, began to arrive. Normally, Purah would sing to herself, for therapy. Today her worship was enhanced.

While in bed, she swayed with the rhythm of her song. First, she was humming, then a curtsy, then raising her grasping hand, "Precious Lord"[20]. It was so clear. Purah's frail body seemed to be moving to a waltz.

---

[20] (Dorsey 1938)

As she hummed, David sang the words, adding the embellishments.

Then stopping the waltz, she stared out the window into the distance, singing.

Then, humming...

Focused and in deep thought, Purah whispered, "In Christ alone." Then drifted into a restful sleep.

You would often hear her whisper "In Christ alone" as she was ministering to others, whether welcoming the Harbor Oak guests or in her volunteer days. It was a watchword for her, closing personal notes and letters, using those very words.

CHAPTER SEVEN
The Note

Most mornings began with coffee at the Gideons' home.

"Ochre, I'm not moving," said Scruffy, contending for his chair.

Ochre scooped him up and whispered, "Go play in the street."

It was Ochre's unofficial duty to bring the sad news about Rose's untimely death. "I am completely devastated," he said. "This is something we could have never imagined."

"I can clearly see that the battle is now defined." If no one else knew, Miller understood. "Gideon was chosen by the Lord that day in the grove to lead this weak crew of aged elderly, into an adoption battle. Gideon of all people. Congestive heart failure—and already in his own battle."

Miller, crossing his arms with fist under chin, "If a battle, then who would be the adversary to this Parenting Paradox?"

Quietly, prayer began. This was a prayer of intercession for Charity Grace. With so many unknowns, the Oaks felt they were called to stand in the gap for her.

"The stakes are immeasurable. Charity Grace's future will hang on much of what we do," said Miller.

Reverend Gideon began the meeting in a decisive manner. "We all believed Rose was feeling confused. She was in a state of shock and grief, knowing she needed to place her baby for adoption. There were probably feelings of fear and denial."

"Purah just found a note from Rose," said Gid. "It is now apparent, she left it the day she left Charity Grace with us. It was between the bath towels in our linen closet."

Feeling unsettled, "Purah, baby, read the note."

"'I am so afraid for my baby. We just cannot raise another child. My husband does not work often. We have seven children in school and two at home. I want you good folks to do what is best for my baby girl. She needs your insight. I just want more for her.'"

"There was no doubt, Rose left her baby with the intensions of us Oaks adopting her," said Gid.

Looking heavenward, "Lord, I know that you know the end from the beginning. I know, this is your *orders* you spoke of, to me in the Harbor Oaks Grove, last Wednesday," said Gid.

Ochre injected, "We need legal counsel."

Ochre was thinking, *I need wiggle room. Adoption is a good idea, but this is not what I would plan. Not at all what I planned.*

Dr. Morrison said, "She needs a birth certificate. Rose must have given birth to her somewhere alone. I will check at the hospitals to confirm that."

Purah said, "Charity Grace's father possesses the right to know about her."

"So, to the important question at hand," said Gid, "what do we believe Rose meant by her statement? 'Call her Charity Grace.' That sounded like her goodbye."

"Let's all pray today and meet again first thing in the morning." Gid could see on the Oaks' faces that they were unprepared for this turn of events. Although they all knew they had daily prayed for guidance, each one was convinced they had passed the baton when it came to strategy for decision making.

Gid was discerning of people and their physiological clues.

There is more going on with Ochre than health problems. He appears obsessed with something. I'm not so sure it is Charity Grace either, thought Gid.

Ochre turned his entire body to gaze at Charity Grace as he scrutinized her features, then a frozen dead stare interrupted as he contemplated the effect of his mandate. Or was it guilt?

Miller's little Scruffy looked up at Ochre and said, *don't even think of it.*

David thought he heard Ochre say, "Mind your own business, Scruffy."

Ochre slipped him a treat and he bounded up Ochre like a ladder onto the back of the chair.

"Ochre, so what did you give him?" asked David.

"If I tell you, I'll have to shoot you."

David gave Ochre a pleading look.

"All right, it was truth serum, but don't tell anybody."

"Did you really?"

#

Erratic thoughts rushed into Ochre's mind. *Guardianship is not something we have any control or authority over, or do we? Family Services needs to be involved,* he thought.

My childhood home may have been much different if Social Services had been involved. It is absurd to even wonder what we thought Rosie meant. We were just meeting her temporary need. She didn't know she was sick or dying. Did she?

Then Ochre said, "Uh, yes, I will pray for Charity Grace tonight."

He narrowed his eyes and pursed his lips while thinking, *After I take care of my report to Family Services.*

Scruffy said, *Ochre, what is your real motivation for this?*

"Somebody tell Scruffy to *shuhut* up," as he feebly made his way out.

#

Ochre's instincts kicked in. At the office, "Suzanne, may I make a personal phone call?"

Phoning the department, "Because I am a mandated reporter, I must inform you, anonymously, a newborn is left in the care of Reverend Gideon at Harbor Oaks Assisted Living. It was learned today that the mother passed away. That is all." Taking a deep breath while gritting his teeth, he hung up. Thru opened mouth, he exhaled in relief, with a quiet groan.

As he walked out the office door, struggling to keep his balance he muttered, "I had no other choice."

#

Ochre immediately headed to the kitchen, looking around to be sure Nat was alone. "Okay, Nat, what do you know?"

"She knowed what she was doing, Ochre. She had dat beebee here at da home."

"What was she thinking? At our age? We all have one foot in the grave, Nat!"

"Anyway, she was skeered for da beebee."

"Did she know she was dying?"

"Yeah, her sugar done got tangled up."

"Okay, then where is Mr. Taylor?"

"Jail right now, but he be out soon.

"Ochre, I dun see, dis is all fur da bes. Gideons will mek a good home. Rose dun thot it out."

"Nat, this is more complicated than you know. Nat, who all knows about this?"

"We all know, Ochre."

"What else do you know, Nat?"

"Rose dun tol me all about it."

"You know how to keep your mouth shut? Yeah, yeah, I know you do."

CHAPTER EIGHT
The Prayer Tower

People would stop by mornings just to hear Miller pray.

Maude heard a knocking. "Look who's here. Come in, Suzanne. Come in and sit down. Have a cup of coffee, dear."

"Thank you, Ms. Maude."

"Ms. Maude, I just felt drawn today to come listen to Miller pray. His prayers are such an encouragement to me."

"My dear, you certainly may," said Maude.

The Waits' apartment had been buzzing all morning. With the local people bringing their prayer needs to Miller, in the "Prayer Tower," he was kept busy most days, interceding for their need.

"Suzanne, when Miller prays, the community takes notice. The prayer room door opens out into the foyer area upstairs. As soon as he goes up those stairs, he throws open the window facing the Harbor Oaks Park and falls on his face.

"You can hear the prayers echoing across the lawn and resonating through the sturdy oaks, then against the river on their way to the very throne room of God."

"It seems as if his prayers are escorted by angels," said Suzanne.

"That's right, into the Holy of Holies in Heaven," said Maude.

"Miller is a man after God's own heart, Suzanne. His experiences have taught him powerful lessons about having an intimate relationship with Jesus, the Lover of His Soul.

"Just listen, he always begins with strands of adoration and praise."

"Jesus," said Miller, "You are the one who went into that Holy of Holies in Heaven with your own blood to make atonement for all my sin. You loved me so much, you sacrificed yourself for my sin, everyone's sin."

"Suzanne, he doesn't waste any time. With fervor, he gradually recalls God's blessings in his life."

Miller continuing, "Lord, I first experienced that intimacy with you as a four-year-old child, whose mother was taken away to the tuberculosis asylum. Oh, how I longed for Mama's arms to wrap around me and make me feel secure.

"Hunger was my constant companion. It was hard times. I know they were common in every family during those days.

"Dad was so overcome with worry about feeding the family and caring for the six-month-old twins. I spent many a night crying into my pillow with no one to comfort me. I prayed, 'God, please bring my mama home.'"

#

"Suzanne, finally, his grandmother Sophie moved in with them. She found time to play with Miller and nurture him, as well as the rest of the children. She taught him to make toys from sticks and barrel hoops. Miller's mother never came home, again.

"Miller took to the farmyard animals and began to herd them, for his dad. That old mare Dolly made a good roping horse. She made a good riding horse and anything else Miller could find to do with her.

She hung with him like a guard dog. His dad made the kids a wagon, and Miller hitched old Dolly to it.

"Dolly met with a tragic accident when she broke her leg. The wagon slid up over her as they went downhill. His dad had to go back and shoot her on the spot. The family all had a funeral for old Dolly. They sang 'In the Sweet By and By,'[21] and carried bouquets of flowers to her grave. There is a cross marking her grave, on the side of River Street, to this day."

"Yeah, I have seen that marker," said Suzanne.

Maude said, "Folks pass by that spot and think some important person is buried there. They even wanted to put a historical marker there back when the Boy Scouts were cleaning up the town," she chuckled.

Suzanne commented, "Miller suffered a lot of adversity in his life."

"Yes, he learned to make that adversity a platform for the gospel.

"After Dolly died, Miller began to have a lot of questions about death.

"He was always looking for something to fill his emptiness. Granny Sophie was good to Miller and helpful with homework, but the pain was still in his heart.

"Finally, one day he had a schoolteacher, Mr. Weeks, who began to take an interest in him. He started taking Miller to church. By that time, Miller was about eight years old. He was beginning to understand this life was not the end for someone who made Jesus Lord of their life.

"Mr. Weeks said, "Miller, Jesus can take the pain in your heart away.'

---

[21] (Bennett and (m.). 1868)

67

"Jesus became Miller's faithful friend. Miller learned how to please Jesus and call on him for guidance. He made himself a prayer loft in the barn, then went around asking folks, 'How can I pray for you or your family?'

"Mrs. Weeks,[22] taught him how to "pickle" pigs' feet. I remember on cold mornings, (that was hog killing weather,) you would hear a knock at the door."

Knock. "Missy Maude," said Miller. "You folks rendering hogs soon? Don't forget me. I need your pig's feet."

"Miller made a sign. "Pickled Pigs' Feet. Ten Cents a bucket." That was his way to get to talk to people. With a little conversation, Miller would say, "I'll be praying for you tonight. Ya got anything you want me to mention?"

"Oh, I remember, even as a child, I could hear Miller in that old treehouse a praying. Our farm was down below theirs in the holler. Hearing a child pray like that gave our community so much comfort. We all began to want what Miller had. How a humble little boy like that could affect so many adults was a real mystery. Miller just knew that his prayers were heard, and he never stopped praying."

"That next summer, after the farmers laid by their crops, the traveling evangelist, Preacher Woods, came through with his wife and dog in an old rickety wagon, and preached our annual revival. People were professing their faith in Jesus.

"Things started happening." Maude threw her head back and laughed. "They were throwing away their rabbit's feet, their horseshoes, and pouring out their liquor. The gambling houses were having to shut their doors. Many of them said they wanted what Miller had. Those prayers had lodged in people's hearts. They wanted the peace that he had found.

---

[22] (Etta Mae Dunn Weeks May 14, 1908-March 21, 1998)

"After that, the men met and cleaned out a spot we called 'The Island,' at the river, for baptism. We would spend the afternoon there, cutting steps into the clay, down the bank, dragging logs out of the path, and of course swinging from the vines in the trees—then having some cold watermelon the boys had stolen from somebody's patch.

"Baptism was always a big event in our community. We only had it one time a year after revival. Folks that got saved during the year might have died and gone to hell, if they didn't know it was their faith in Jesus that saved them—not baptism.

Maude looks up with a far-away expression as though she could see what she described. "My heart is still knitted to that place. I remember that morning, it was raining, and we were sure we would have to postpone the baptism. We just started out walking, though. The older folks and mothers with small children rode in the wagons. By the time we got to the baptizin' hole, the rain had stopped, and the sun was peeping through the clouds. Old Brother Woods said, 'God is smiling on us today.'

"Even that morning you could hear Miller praying through the trees. He would just make himself an altar anywhere. Any old log would do.

Making eye contact with Suzanne, "now, where was I? So, we all gathered, and as the candidates started walking down the slippery bank into the water, we started singing, 'Hark! I Hear the Harps Eternal,'[23] with that sweet four-part a cappella harmony echoing to the heavens." Maude began to look up, fixing her eyes on something, "by that time, the sun was streaking through those stately oak trees. Oh, what a glorious display."

Maude was visibly moved as she related the story. "Suzanne, that vision will be with me until the day I die. The Lord was all around that place. Zion Baptist Church brought glory to God that day.

---

[23] (Parker 1967)

"As they say, in my mind's eye, I can see, Brother Woods, down in that river with his right hand raised to the heavens saying, 'Upon your profession of faith in the Lord Jesus Christ, and in obedience to the Lord's command, I baptize you my sister in the name of the Father, Son and Holy Ghost. You are buried in the likeness of his death and raised in the likeness of His resurrection.'"

Wiping tears from her eyes, Suzanne said, "Maude, how I would love to experience something like that."

Just then, Miller walked into the room with his long flowing white handkerchief, still wiping the tears.

"Oh, Miller." Suzanne was standing now, as she reached to hug him. "Hearing you pray with such intensity and passion gives me new meaning to what prayer is all about. I must be going, though."

Miller said, "Tell me how's your mama and 'nem?"

After she told Miller all about Mama and Daddy's ailments, Miller said, "Baby, you know I pray for you every day."

"Do you really? That touches my heart, Miller."

"Yes, are there any needs in your life I can be praying about?"

CHAPTER NINE
DFS Visit.

"Gid," said Purah, "this child may have never seen a doctor. I am taking her now to see Doc Edmond. We can't wait for this meeting. I will be back as quickly as possible."

"When Purah makes up her mind, she gets things done."

Just as she was going out the door, in walked their neighbor, Dr. Morrison.

"Purah, I was able to get what they call a provisional birth certificate, only because I am a medical doctor. There are some legalities that need to be addressed, especially that of finding out the name of Charity Grace's father."

"Thank you, Doctor, I can see God's hand in this. I will need it for her to see the pediatrician."

"Gid, give me that note that Rose left. Without it, I don't have any legal right to obtain her health care."

Purah was off in a flash.

#

Just as the meeting was about to start, a stranger approached Gid's front door. He looked to be in a certain kind of official capacity. There was another person getting out of the car, a woman carrying a briefcase.

The Oaks had gathered including Doc Morrison's wife, who had retired after many years of being a successful trial attorney. They lived a quiet life, seeming to enjoy their retirement. Their jobs were both of an intense nature. Now, they took the time with one another as though they were newlyweds. They walked every morning and evening, and you often saw them holding hands.

Hugging everyone as though she hadn't seen them in years, Maude said, "Tell me about your recent doctor visit. Update me on those grand and great-grandchildren."

Miller said, "Praise reports are coming in for answered prayer. Y'all keep me updated, so I'll know how to pray."

Miller and Maude brought Scruffy in his doggie/baby stroller. He was always a welcomed guest. Everyone pet him as though he was a lucky charm. That dog seemed to know what people were thinking. You would believe he was human, the way people talked to him.

Ochre came in walking with stiff joints and looking like he had a long night. He looked over at Scruffy, scooting on the rug, then hopping up into his chair.

"Scruffy, you got my seat again. Scoot over."

He seemed to hear Scruffy say, "You need to loosen up, Ochre."

Ochre looked over at Maude. "Did you hear that?"

He scooped Scruffy up and put him up on his shoulder, whispering in his ear, "You are not still eating your poop are you, Scruffy?"

David had given Ochre the nickname 'The Dog Whisperer,' while always so curious as to what Ochre would whisper into Scruffy's ear. He made a point to sit next to where Ochre sat, and this time he leaned over toward him. "Ochre, did you just say what I thought you said?"

"David, Scruffy said 'he saved you some.'"

David rolled his lip up and gave Ochre a cheesy toothless grin.

"Here, David, wear these," said Ochre.

"What? Those are your dry-sitting teeth."

"Yeah, where are we going this year?" said David.

"We can't miss the reaction of those kids when they see us. Let's sit outside the grocery store Friday," said David.

"I have a better idea. Let's go to the school cafeteria and sit on the haybales outside. It is getting harder and harder to sit without moving. I better practice this year," said Ochre.

Ochre said, "No, Scruffy, you can't go—you can't be still."

#

Then came the knock on the door. Weldon with his nylon dress shirt and robin's egg blue socks that his daughter gave him made his crew-cut hardly noticeable. Vermillia was carrying a box brief case that seemed to be important, but no one knew because she never opened it. Her hair was in a tight ball, probably to keep from getting lice in undesirable homes. She wore a shirtwaist dress with socks and penny loafers. Her face was emotionless.

"Reverend Gideon, my name is Weldon, and this is Vermillia. We are social workers for the Department of Family Services." Looking around at the group gathered in the room, "Is there somewhere we can go to have a private conversation?"

Reverend Gideon responded, "These are our lifelong friends, and we all live here at Harbor Oaks. We call ourselves the Oaks." Our relationship is that of a family. I believe that it would be advisable to allow them all to remain."

"Very well. A report made to the department stated, 'You are caring for an abandoned child.' Is that correct?"

"Weldon, we do have an infant—my wife and me. She was left in our care. They are not here now. My wife took her to the pediatrician for a wellness checkup. We learned of the death of the newborn, Charity Grace's mother, Rose Taylor, just night before last. We all spent the day yesterday in prayer for Charity Grace. Rose is or was our personal care attendant, here at the home."

"Where is the child's father, Reverend Gideon?"

"Sir, it is an unfortunate fact that we do not know the answer. The mother informed us before Charity Grace's birth that the father, her husband, did not know that she was pregnant with their tenth child."

Weldon and Vermillia looked at one another and rolled their eyes.

Gid continued, "You see, she had planned to never tell him. He is an alcoholic who does not work. She was the only source of income for the family. She had asked us to help her pray about what to do. We all agreed to pray, and she left."

"So how, Reverend Gideon, did you come to have custody of this child, may I say, at your age?"

"Rose brought the baby to work with her. When she came to our apartment, she had hidden Charity Grace on her housekeeping cart. We did not know that the baby had been born. Rose was out sick the day before, and we were all concerned.

"Rose asked us to keep Charity Grace that night to give her time to make some plans. She didn't return to work the next day. The weekend passed and then two more days, still no Rose. We contacted our executive director, and she learned that Rose had died. It was about that time that Purah found the note last evening that Rose left."

"Oh, I am beginning to see a plan. So, you have a note?"

"Yes, Purah found where it was hidden in the stack of bath towels. We were all so stunned, our Oaks decided to have a meeting this morning.

"Dr. Morrison said he would take care of getting Charity Grace a birth certificate. He just told us he was only able to get a provisional birth certificate because the father is currently unknown.

"Purah insisted on taking Charity Grace to the pediatrician first thing this morning. So, here we are, and here you are. Purah and Charity Grace have not returned yet.

"So, Weldon," said Gid as he took off his glasses and raised one eyebrow, "do you mind if I ask who made this report to the Department of Family Services?"

"Sir, that information is always held in confidence. All we can tell you is what the report said. The report stated, 'An abandoned newborn is at the home of a Reverend Gideon.' There was nothing said incriminating anyone."

"Gid looked around the room. He knew that no one knew about Charity Grace except the Oaks. Thinking back to last night, "Was there any negativity in the room as we were dealing with our shock? Everyone seemed in distress but very calm and engaged. We were getting good response, as we talked about our next steps.

"We had been living our lives for the last week, knowing that God was about to present us with our greatest challenge. Could it be? Is this it? The Lord said we would get our orders soon."

Purah, walking through the door, "What a pleasant surprise. Who are our guests?"

"Allow me to introduce ourselves, Mrs. Gideon. I am Weldon and this is Vermillia. We are with the Department of Family Services. We are following up on a report about a newborn infant in your custody."

Purah cut her eyes in a questioning look. "A report?"

"Purah, what did the pediatrician say?" asked Gid.

Purah began to read, "'Baby girl born approximately three weeks early, a bit underweight, and shows signs of being well cared for. She is healthy, with no need for hospitalization.'

"He even said there are numerous couples waiting to adopt a newborn."

"Reverend Gideon," Weldon said, "it seems this is an unprecedented situation. I will leave Charity Grace with you until the department can find foster care for her. It doesn't seem that she is at risk or that she needs emergency placement. You have shown good faith, in getting her checked out, and even taking steps to get her birth certificate. I will contact you tomorrow to update you and your Oaks about placement for her."

"Weldon, with all due respect to you and your department, do you believe having this handwritten will has bearing on this situation?"

Taking the note, Weldon quickly analyzed it and stated, "Reverend Gideon, that is an unknown. The juvenile judge will most likely have the final say concerning this matter. Surely, you would not attempt to adopt her at your age. The baby's father will now be her guardian."

Nathaniel was coincidentally, intentionally sitting on the Gideons' side patio as DFS was leaving Harbor Oaks Assisted Living. Curiosity was one of his finer points.

Once outside, Weldon stated to his coworker, "This has the makings of some bad press for the department. The public will be extremely interested in how this turns out. The longer it is held in trust, the better for all. It will be made public later, but it needs to be after investigation and the department is able to answer questions."

She responded, "Weldon, is that your primary concern?"

"What's that Vermillia?"

"Bad press."

"Vermillia, at my age, yes. That is a newborn baby. She is obviously being well-cared for. There will be thousands who want her. Unfortunately, we will have little to do with that. Her father will make any decision. The press will be our biggest problem."

As they drove away, Nathaniel said, "Bad press? I be knowing what to do with that."

CHAPTER TEN
The Hindrance Is Gone

A numbness set in as the Oaks began to chat. What, how, who, when. They all knew what the note meant. Seeing it through eyes of faith and knowing how God is not bound by man's inabilities and weaknesses, in God's economy, helplessness does not equal hopelessness.

Reverend Gideon stood from his wheelchair, then acknowledging Miller, "My desire is to invoke the Holy Spirit into the launch of this voyage that will take us into unknown waters."

Everyone in the room fell to their knees.

With his face to the floor, Miller lifted his weak voice to the Heavens. "Oh, Holy Father, we need you now. We need your guidance. We need your Holy Spirit to strengthen us for our task ahead."

You could hear weeping all over the room. Choruses in holy harmony of agreement, with moans and amens, reverberating throughout the room.

"Lord, we believe you will empower us for this divine mission. We are frail and tired, but your strong arm will lead us. You will go before us and prepare the way, where there is no way.

Just as you created the world and all that is in it, out of darkness and nothingness, we believe you will bring into existence a new thing.

Nothing is too hard for you.

In the quietness of this room, we ask that you speak. We ask that your voice well up in us like mighty waters, to refresh our spirits and restore our vigor for the task that lies ahead. In the precious name, the name above every name, Jesus!"

Ochre looked sick. He leaned forward with eyes crossed, then he whispered, "God, I can't do this anymore."

The silence was saturated with worshipful moans, and many continued to pray.

The room grew cold as a dark, greenish, indistinct shadow emerged out from behind and moved slowly across the room. The figure was as though it was three fused forms. The creature made its way across the room, reeking with a putrid odor and then disappearing through the outside wall.

Ochre was fanning his face and running his fingers through his hair.

"The hindrance is gone," said Gid. "Full steam ahead."

"Thank you, Miller. His prayer recalls the Word, in Isaiah 43:18-19. Purah, read this please."

Remember ye not the former things, neither consider the things of old. Behold, I will do a new thing; now it shall spring forth; shall ye not know it? I will even make a way in the wilderness, and rivers in the desert.[24]

"This is just what we need!" said Gid. "It has been a long night. Already this morning, much is accomplished.

---

[24] ((KJV) n.d.)

"Allow me to paraphrase this verse.

"Do not use your past to define the new thing that I am about to do. Observe it springing forth. I am establishing for you a highway in your barrenness with an artesian fountain in what you perceived to be desolation.

"Jeremiah 32:17 says, 'There is nothing too hard for thee.'[25] Purah, will you keep notes for us and help us stay focused?"

Gideon once again stood from his wheelchair, looking beyond the Oaks. "Holy Spirit, we thank you that you will preside over this humble meeting today."

Easing himself into the chair, "I believe our shared desire is to do God's will, to do what is best for Charity Grace. We believe her needs supersede our own.

"Each of you are welcome to speak on this mission, as we wade through the shallow water of facts and launch into the river of what we believe to be our *Closing Life-Challenge.*

"My dearest friends, allow us to begin." Standing again, "understand that *We* Are the *Oaks,* not anxious or fearful."

Dr. Morrison respectfully stood. "Understand, Reverend Gideon, we see ourselves as a family. We are morally obligated to stand with you and Purah, shoulder to shoulder, in this *Closing Life-Challenge.*

"Isaac Newton spoke of, 'Standing on the shoulders of giants.' Those of us in this room *are* giants. Not only are each of us major thinkers, but we also bear on our shoulders others who look to us for guidance.[26] We will launch this *Closing Life-Challenge*, into rough seas. We are about to encounter this *new thing* God is establishing, by His grace," said the doctor.

---

[25] ((KJV) n.d.)
[26] (I. Newton 1643-1727) (Norworth 1908)

Continuing, "Age may be a factor, but it is not the Captain of our souls. We can count the many weaknesses that we bear, but we have the Captain of the Lord's Army to guide us through this battle. We will not fail. Moreover, we must be wise. Let us advance; we can surmise the enemy's tactics. The enemy would have us be fearful.

1. Social Services must find Charity Grace's father.
2. They are bound by law.
3. The father is legally bound to decide her future. We will be at his mercy.
4. I believe he will have no interest in her.
5. Although Charity Grace was left with us today, that is only temporary. The department will put her in approved foster care. Our hope: for her father to grant legal custody to us.
6. We must pray for a quick decision."

"Thank you, Dr. Morrison."

"Ochre, what are your thoughts? I am sure you have a massive body of experience in this department."

Ochre raised one eyebrow and slowly stood as he braced himself. He momentarily froze in an uncomfortable position, as he eased Scruffy to the floor. Ochre was sure of it. He was sure that Scruffy said in an audible voice, "Ochre, tell them what you did."

All the while Ochre was thinking, *this can't be happening. Scruffy, you didn't just talk to me. Did you?*

I am just stressed to the point that it is affecting my mobility, thought Ochre.

"Reverend Gideon, I co concur with Dr. Morrison about the, the, the, uh, Father. He must be found. Um," Ochre stuttered, gritting his teeth. "The child has a father. You are correct, the DFS will place her in foster care. Today is just a gesture of kindness." In the wake of that, Ochre sat down.

"Mrs. Morrison, where do we currently stand legally?"

She looked at Ochre with a quizzical look, "Friends, there are a couple of points we need to pray about...

1. The social worker made a grave error. He should have never mentioned age. Age discrimination is a federal law. I will need to research its bearing on adoption. Federal law trumps all other laws. This error on his part may be a huge factor if it comes to adoption.
2. The father does have absolute rights. However, he can relinquish his rights, either to the State or to someone he chooses.
3. Our best chance to attain the adoption would be to get the father to give us guardianship early on. That way, we would be ready with medical documentation regarding Charity Grace's care and psychological profile, and the home study would be complete by then.
4. Understand that these things take time. We best grasp that now, and we will have smooth sailing.
5. One final thing, our lease agreements state that no *one* under the age of 18 can live here. That *one* would be Charity Grace."

"Thank you, Mrs. Morrison. Miller," said Gid. "What would you like to inject?"

"The Angels in heaven are rejoicing with us today. God is in our presence. We are so humbled by what we have witnessed.

"Most importantly, let's all get a copy of Purah's notes and pray item by item. I would like for us to adjourn to Harbor Oaks Riverfront Park and just meditate and pray."

Reverend Gideon took a deep breath and there was no struggle to breathe. He paused to talk to Purah before walking out. "I believe I feel like walking. My breathing is not labored, and my feet don't seem swelled."

Purah was stunned. "Gid, you have been in the wheelchair for a week now. Your breathing is becoming so labored you are having difficulty sleeping, even with nighttime oxygen."

"Now," said Gid, "how are we going to get Charity Grace to the Oak Grove? We can't carry her."

"We could lay her in your wheelchair, Gid. God always provides. Better still, Miller left Scruffy's stroller." They both laughed. "God does have an astounding sense of humor."

Once under the giant oaks, the Oaks all felt empowered. "This fishy-smelling warm breeze blowing off the water reminds me of my days as a barefoot boy," said Gid. "I would catch mudcats and skin and gut them right here on the peer. I was able to sell them and earn money to buy my school shoes in the fall.

"I prayed many a prayer under these oaks. You can do a lot of thinking sitting by the river." Gid recollected the prayer. "Lord, does mama need the money that I will get for these mudcats? I know Daddy can't work and we have bills to pay. I might be able to get by till winter without shoes.

"Purah, read me the list, item by item. We will pray and go on to the dining room, then rest a little before bedtime."

As Reverend Gideon and Purah walked, Gid commented, "Purah, I believe Ochre is showing symptoms of Parkinson's. Did you notice in the meeting, he had that frozen movement? His neck is so stiff, and today he is stuttering. His right hand was shaking when they walked outside."

"I did notice all that, but I was wondering if he might be the one that made the report to the department. Living with that would be unnerving, even if he had dealt with that sort of thing for a living. His advice was more matter-of-fact. He didn't seem to be committed to our purpose."

"Purah, I have great respect for your discerning spirit. We never know what devices Satan will use to thwart God's plan. I know this seems absurd, but God will make a way, in this wilderness.

"Let's not mention our observations about Ochre to anyone. The kind thing to do would be wait and be sure. My daddy always said, 'There is always a possibility that we could be wrong.'"

Ochre was unnerved about the meeting. *What is wrong with my body? Why can I not move the way I normally do? Is this situation causing me enough stress to become so debilitated? And what's more, I thought that Scruffy was talking to me.*

Ochre heard the train whistle as it was going through the crossing. *Once again, I am plagued with the horrific memory on that dreadful day.*

All the details came flooding back. *It has been so long ago, but it never leaves me. Our car stalled on the tracks. Oh, I can't relive that again.*

Trying to straighten up he began to walk the winding path from the Harbor Oaks River Park.

I would have benefitted from counseling, he thought. Counseling was unheard of for children in those days. *Charity Grace should have the benefit of all the social services. I know what is best for her. I know what to do. I will handle this. After all, ...* Then a long pause, "Dear God, what should I do?"

CHAPTER ELEVEN
Loving and Losing Charity Grace

"We will just walk into the dining room as usual. No one will know Charity Grace is in the stroller. They will all think it is Scruffy," said Gid.

"Unca Gid, y'all puppy sitting?" asked Nathaniel with a grin.

Sleep comes easy for a little one, especially with the warm breeze blowing off the river in her face.

"Nathaniel, what have you cooked up for us tonight?" said Gid.

As the Oaks sat around the table, you could feel their excitement about the evening menu.

"Nat, I'm having crackling cornbread and buttermilk tonight," said David.

Ochre, leaning over to David, "I thought you didn't eat pork."

Giving Ochre a cold shoulder, "Nathaniel, I'll have cornbread and buttermilk tonight."

David whispered in a quick outburst, "Ochre, you know I can't eat it now that you have told me that."

"Studying the menu, I think I want a fried bologna sandwich, with a slab of hoop cheese—on the side," said Mrs. Morrison. "This place goes overboard to provide us what we like."

"Unca Gid," said Nathaniel, you be looking like Hollywood tonight. You must be feelin' betta."

"Nathaniel, my breathing is much better, thank you."

#

Gid and Purah retired to their apartment with Charity Grace, as a new family that faced insurmountable obstacles.

"Gid, we would have never dreamed that God would give us such a battle," Purah said. "This is a battle not only regarding adoption by an aged couple—it seems to be one fought on so many fronts. Who in their right mind would take on this task? Yet we both feel passionately about God's plan?"

"Baby, I just feel the peace of God flowing through me tonight, a peace that will yield remarkable fruit. Somehow, I feel Him impressing me to end our evening reading, Hebrews 12.[27] The devoted Patriarchs in the Old Testament were honored by God for their faithfulness, because their faith pleased Him."

Gid slept without his oxygen that night.

When he awakened, he lay there rehearsing in his mind the most recent events. He was thinking, *all our plans and actions must be as though God's promises are not just imminent, but that they have already transpired. Our faith will produce substance.*

"Lord, I can almost see Charity Grace in the different stages of her life. She will be skilled in all manner of abilities and graces. You have a plan to use her to honor your purpose."

---

[27] ((KJV) n.d.)

#

He did not hear Charity Grace cry during the night. "Purah, how is 'Sweet Baby Girl'?"

"She slept good, was up twice for feeding and changing, and is asleep again."

Gid and Purah talked to her continuously.

"Gid, you know David comes over and sings to her. All the while he moves her hands as though she is conducting the orchestra, and her feet as though she is dancing. He puts her hand on his throat while he sings to feel his vocal cords vibrate. She is already making imitative sounds."

"Purah, I have to admit, I am smitten with the way she remains focused on your every word and then falls off to sleep in exhaustion. All that exertion is what makes her sleep so well at night."

They were off to the follow-up doctor appointment. Dr. Edmonds was amazed at her attention span. Looking back at his notes from her last visit, he remarked, "Her progress far exceeds expectations."

"Doctor, I believe I need your observations in writing, for the State worker."

"I will do better than that. I will give you graphs that show her progress along with comparisons on standard expectations. Do you need anything else, Purah?"

"Yes, would you write a letter for the judge, recommending us for temporary custody, until this is settled?"

#

Each of the Oaks came over every day, spending time with Charity Grace. She became so accustomed to their appointments that she became fretful if the Oaks overslept their own naps. Dr. Morrison would exercise her, almost as though she were doing pushups. He made games of the movement, using music and rhythms, waiting for

89

her to respond appropriately. He would laugh in an animated way that taught her to do the same. Charity Grace's playtime was a workout.

Together, Pansie and Charity Grace would watch baseball. Pansie taught her the umpire motions as the game would progress. Rehearsing them, "Show me a strike, a ball, a fair ball, and an out." Laughing, then eating their Cracker Jacks, and singing, "Take Me Out to the Ball Game,"[28] all the while oblivious to their surroundings.

Everyone was falling in love with her more every day. No one could bear the thought of losing her to foster care.

#

"This is a dreadful day, Vermillia," said Purah, with the department showing up at the Gideons' door with documents stating that Charity Grace was going into foster care tomorrow.

"Pack her possessions and have them ready to go with her at 10 a.m.," said Vermillia.

For some reason, this came as an abrupt surprise. Each of the Oaks responded with untold emotion.

"We cannot allow this to happen," said Maude. "We weren't even able to have a hearing."

#

Mrs. Morrison filed a brief at 9 a.m. the next morning, requesting an injunction from the juvenile judge. Judge Thomas ruled in favor of the State but set a hearing date. Then Vermillia came to the Gideon home and took Charity Grace from weeping frail arms, with the remaining Oaks lining the walkway. The social worker's face was emotionless and professional. She was very matter-of-fact in her

---

[28] (Norworth 1908)

instruction. She informed Gid and Purah that they would have visitation three days a week.

When asked about the rest of the Oaks' visitation, she said, "The judge will determine that."

Dr. Morrison conversed with the Oaks. "My concern for her bonding to us, and then being torn away, will be unhealthy emotionally for her."

The foster parents were well trained and kind to her, as their hopes were to be able to adopt her.

Vermillia made her visit to the new foster home and said, "Yes, she is bonded to those old folks and is accustomed to their daily visits. Charity Grace is not faring well here."

Vermillia learned from the foster parents, "Her routine has been so interrupted, to the point she cries all the time, and she will not eat or drink."

Dr. Edmonds determined, "She is losing too much weight and must go back from where she came."

Vermillia managed to cut through some paperwork and get through to the judge.

The judge evaluated all the medical information both before and during the foster care placement. He considered the Oaks' ages, and their living circumstances. The judge stated, "I notice a Home Study is not underway. This child needs permanent placement soon." Still questioning, "Where is the father of Charity Grace?"

Vermillia stated, "Your honor, the department learned that the father is in jail."

"I will place Charity Grace back in the home of Reverend and Purah Gideon, giving them temporary guardianship. At the time the department finds the father, we will finalize this, by terminating his rights or giving him his child. The State Department of Family

Services will advertise in the county legal organ for one month to inform the father, at which time the court will finalize the decision."

CHAPTER TWELVE
Gid's Good Report

As was David's habit, he went down to the park with his flute, where he meditated best. His heart still throbbed from the loss of his wife and only son. Now, there was so much to comprehend about the battle that was raging.

Sitting on his usual bench, he opened the case, took out the flute, and polished it, while he was envisioning Charity Grace playing a lyrical movement in his chamber orchestra.

Next, he lay it down and took the mouthpiece and meticulously polished it, carefully inspecting it as he had so many times.

Putting the mouthpiece on the flute he said to himself, "This thing feels heavier than usual."

Bringing it to his mouth, gently and methodically, he inhaled slowly, then exhaled, relaxing as he did.

Now placing his mouth on the mouthpiece, he inhaled again, and gently began to blow.

"PbaPbaPba."

"It sounds like a reed instrument with vibrato…. What was that?"

Something was vibrating inside that mouthpiece like a whoopee cushion.

Thinking something was loose in the mouthpiece itself, he took it off. Then he peered inside and jumped as though it exploded in his face.

A hatchling snake had crawled into his flute. Now, David did not know if that creature was poisonous or non-poisonous. He just slung it out, grabbed the case, and ran across the lawn like an ostrich with its tail feathers on fire.

Ochre saw David coming. "Where are you going? Your feet are running ahead of you. Is that a fancy new dance step?"

"Okay, Mr. Know-it-all, I need snake advice."

"I assure you that was a nonpoisonous snake, David. Sorry to laugh, but that is sidesplitting," and they both had a good belly laugh. "I can see you now, slinging that snake out of that flute, hehehehe."

"We better be headed over to the Gideons. We might be missing out," said Ochre.

David related his snake story to the Oaks, and they all laughed so hard. Little Charity Grace gave her first cackle. That caused them all to laugh the more, with proper Mrs. Morrison giving a good snort. Then she wet her pants.

With temporary guardianship, the Oaks seemed to relax for a while. Gid told the Oaks, "I never thought I would feel this good again. My home nurse is coming today. I wonder what she will think."

#

With intensity, Ochre said, "David, I am off to my skydiving lesson. See you in the funny papers."

Ochre was muttering to himself. *Is this the best way? I don't want anyone to feel responsible. I don't want it to look like suicide. Crashing my plane wouldn't work—they would know that was no accident—but a novice skydiving accident would not be suspicious. I just need to be sure my instructor doesn't look negligent. Or maybe a snakebite?*

#

A Harbor Oaks Assisted Living social function brought Purah's hospitality talents to the forefront. She was welcoming everyone with that sweet personal touch, then she saw Gid's Hospice nurse, who often carried out activities for the residents. "Well, good afternoon, Nurse Cathy. Is there something I can help you with? Let me offer you some sweet, iced tea. What will we be doing today?"

"We have set up a silhouette booth. Later your silhouettes will be posted. The contest allows the other residents and their families to guess who is who. That always creates interesting conversation and encourages families to interact with one another."

"Cathy, your girls always come up with such thought-provoking activities for us here, at the assisted living home. It sure helps to keep us high-functioning."

"Purah, I wish there were something more we could do for Reverend Gideon. I will be over to see him this afternoon. We will go over some things you will experience. You need to know what to expect."

"Cathy, this appointment is of great interest to both Gid and myself."

Purah had so many thoughts on her mind. Charity Grace of course, and then there was Gid. *I just don't know what to make of his improvement.*

#

"Gid, Nurse Cathy said she would be here later this afternoon. She wants to go over some of the things you can expect to experience— through this-this uh time?"

"Just watch, Babe, I believe she will be astonished, when she sees me."

Cathy and Connie, her co-worker approached the door, Cathy raised her hand to the doorbell, "Connie, what is that?"

In a powerful baritone voice, Gid was belting out his worship and praise. "Bless the Lord, Oh my soul, and all that is within me, bless His Holy Name. Ps. 103:1"[29]

Purah opened the door. "Y'all come in. Forgive me for my southern charm today—I'm feeling completely ecstatic."

Connie commented, "Whatever for?" Cutting her eyes at Cathy, "This is your home."

Cathy said, "Purah and Reverend Gideon, this is Connie, our Hospice social worker."

Gideon, reaching for her hands, in a jovial mood, remarked, "What can we do for you today?"

Cathy cut *her* eyes to Connie, then questioningly raised her eyebrows.

"Reverend Gideon, this type of Hospice visit is always difficult for the family, with discussions of signs of the end, etc."

Nurse Cathy, noticing how unlabored his breathing was, toned down her approach. "We are just here for a routine visit. I will start with getting your vitals. Your respiration is improved, Reverend Gideon. It is near normal. Now tell me just who taught you to sing like that?"

Pumping the blood pressure cuff. "Your blood pressure is normal. Now, let me listen to your breathing." As she warmed the stethoscope,

------

[29] ((KJV) n.d.)

she was puzzled, thinking back through her notes. "Take a deep breath and cough."

His diagnosis was confirmed by two doctors, she thought.

"Your lungs are clear, Gid. What different have you been doing? Hm, let me look at your medication.

"Don't take your blood pressure medicine in the morning, and you better hold off on that diuretic."

After assessing his medication, diet, fluid intake, and vitals, she told Gid, "The Hospice doctor will be coming by for a routine visit tomorrow. We will go ahead today and draw blood so he will have the results when he comes."

Connie commented, "Congratulations on your good report today, Reverend Gideon. It was so good to meet you both."

"Ms. Cathy, you asked what I've been doing differently. God is giving me a new commission. This is an unorthodox battle for one my age. We have been granted guardianship of a newborn baby. We are working toward adopting her."

"Reverend Gideon, I am speechless. This is certainly unprecedented. I am sure there is a backstory to this. I want to hear all about it on my next visit. You folks get a good night's sleep tonight."

As they left, the social worker said, "That was interesting. And how old is he?"

"My records say he is seventy-five years old."

CHAPTER THIRTEEN
Live Encounter News

The reporters from the local TV station stepped out of their car onto the sidewalk. Chuck the broadcaster—a homegrown young man, surviving on nasal spray and jellybeans—spun around in awe and said, "Look at this place. These old folks have finally arrived. This place looks like a resort. Get a load of this view, Chris."

"I believe a woman runs this place, Chris. I don't know whether to knock or walk in." Knock, Knock, Knock. "Mrs. Suzanne Josephson?"

"Yes, what can I do to help you?"

"Allow me, Mrs. Josephson. My name is Chuck Converse, and this is my co-worker Chris. Lighthouse Encounter Broadcasting learned that there is an elderly couple here in Harbor Oaks who is hoping to adopt a newborn infant. Our TV station is interested in an interview with them."

"That is remarkable, Mr. Converse. I can't help you. I have no such knowledge."

Suzanne stood, walked over, and put her hand on the doorknob.

"This is precisely the type of human-interest story we believe the community would be very fascinated in learning all about. It is a gripping thought, you know. How old would they be when the child starts school, plays sports, or graduates? We could follow this story for years, if there are years."

"You could be right. However, I am afraid that I cannot help you." Then Suzanne opened the door to show them out.

With reluctance, he walked out the door, then turning to face her. "Look, our station is prepared to make it worth your while, as soon as possible.

"This would really boost our ratings. Our advertisers would be scrambling for spots. Think about it, Mrs. Josephson. It will create interest about your residence too.

"Here is my card, Mrs. Josephson. My personal contact information is there. I will be waiting to hear from you."

Walking out onto the sidewalk, Chuck tried to be cordial to residents who were out for their stroll. He was surprised that he was uncomfortable talking to this generation.

"I wonder if they can hear me," he asked Chris, his cameraman.

They were all giving him the once-over, even looking over their shoulder as they passed.

"Do you fellers know anything about an adoption around here?"

Chuck chuckled as he overheard one of them say, "Does he think we are deaf?"

The walking partner wheezed out a laugh. "I may not be able to hear, but I can smell, and I smell a rat. Hehehe."

"Come on, Chris," Chuck said. "Let's head out there to Harbor Oaks River Park. What a view, and it is wasted on these old folks."

"Why do they paint the darn trees white, Chuck?"

"Probably a good reason. These folks know more than we will ever know.

"Chris, People this age have gained a sixth sense. It is rare that they offer any information to strangers, even if they know something.

"I want to just walk around and get a feel for this place."

Walking under the spreading oaks, "There is something. Do you feel it? There is a lot of history here, a lot of energy. I feel a presence here. Let's get out of here."

Chris: "The only person who would even talk to us referred to some teacher these old folks had sixty years ago. Make a note— 'scooter man' and 'teacher'?

"This is a priceless story. We have got to make it worth their while to weigh in on our probes. Everybody knows seniors love freebies."

"So, what can we offer them?" Chris asked.

"I know," said Chuck, "something to do with scooters."

"Now we are getting somewhere. Suppose we create riding trails for them here in the park, Chris? I will get the LE News marketers working on this today. Wow, I am brilliant. Any nugget of information can turn into a gold mine."

"Let's show up out here again tomorrow. We will become a familiar face to these old folks."

CHAPTER FOURTEEN
God Uses Weak Things

The Hospice doctor is to pay you a visit today, Gid."

"Huh. I can't help but wonder what he will do. Will he take me off Hospice?"

"Gid, what kind of man does this kind of doctoring? All his patients die."

Gid threw his head back laughing, "Not this one, not now," said Gid. "That must be him pulling into the driveway. Give him your classic welcome, Purah."

"Come in, Doctor. We have been expecting your visit. We appreciate your coming. How in the world are you? I know you are so busy to be spending time with us."

As he walked through the door, he nodded at Mrs. Gideon. "Thank you, Madam. My name is Ben Solomon."

In a very matter of fact tone, "I have come to make a medical call on Reverend Gideon. I am told by Nurse Cathy he is showing some improvement."

Purah gave him that Cheshire cat grin and brought him into the parlor. "We may be experiencing a miracle, Doctor."

Extending his hand, "Reverend Gideon, I am your Hospice doctor, Benjamin Solomon."

"It's my pleasure, Doctor."

"You can call me Ben."

"Ben? You have two biblical names."

"Yes, Benjamin LaMar Solomon."

"Ben, 'Son of LaMar, Solomon?"

"Reverend Gideon, I have never thought of it that way." *Son of LaMar, LaMarah.*

Purah laughed. "Dr. Solomon, Gid puts things into perspective."

I am going to meditate on that, thought Reverend Gideon. *Son of LaMar, Son of LaMarah.*

#

"As you know, Reverend, once a patient is on Hospice, they will no longer see their primary care physician. I will see you here, at your home, and you have a home nurse making visits.

"Nurse Cathy tells me you have made some improvement."

"That I have, Doctor. I am feeling much better. I guess you will want to check me out and see for yourself."

Placing the stethoscope to Gid's chest, "Take a deep breath, Reverend Gideon, and hold it. Uh-huh. Now, I want to check your vitals. Let me see your feet," not acknowledging the obvious improvement.

"What changed since your diagnosis?" all the while studying Gid's lack of puffiness in his face and neck, his unlabored breathing, his ability to carry on normal-paced conversation, and his normal O_2.

"Doctor, I realize, what I am about to tell you makes little sense."

"Reverend Gideon, I am very interested in knowing."

"My improvement is a phenomenon with little explanation except that it is the powerful healing hand of God. You see, God impressed me with a battle to fight, with specific instructions from the Lord."

"You say, a battle? What on earth do you mean? I didn't know preachers fought battles."

"When I received his battle plan, Ben, I was ready to obey Him, because I had prayed for His guidance regarding the enduring legacy I would be leaving behind. It is not that we haven't made waves in our areas of expertise, Doc.

"Doctor, one thing I have learned in my lifetime is that you do not 'put your hand to the plow and then look back.' Luke 9:62.[30] I have been doing the Lord's work a long time and I am often surprised at my assignments.

"During my prayer by the river, the Lord spoke in my spirit. He said I had been a 'Valiant Warrior' and he had one *Closing Life-Challenge* for me. He then said that I would receive my orders soon. Doctor, my orders are to take this child, Charity Grace, and raise her, pouring my life experience into her."

"No one can deny, it is a surprise," commented Dr. Solomon, shaking his head.

Gid continued, "After our meeting there under the oak trees, I preached that same evening and disclosed the *Closing Life-Challenge* to our Crew—we now call Oaks.

"Rose Taylor, our personal care attendant, shared that evening at our home her dilemma. 'Pregnant with her tenth child,' she was planning to give it up for adoption."

---

[30] ((KJV) n.d.)

"Rose asked us to watch her, immediately after she was born. She said she needed some time to make some plans. Overnight turned into days. She did not return. We learned of her death and then found her handwritten will, regarding Charity Grace.

"The others in our group have also taken up this gauntlet. You see, Dr. Solomon, we have prayed that God would take our offering of our life experiences and create an enduring legacy. That legacy will be and is being bestowed upon this infant baby girl.

"There is a pattern and I have seen it frequently. "God hath chosen the weak things of the world to confound the things which are mighty" 1 Cor 1:27.[31]

"I'm not following you," said Dr. Solomon. "Weak things?"

"There is no denying, we are frail and aged. 'God will strongly support those whose heart is completely His'" 2 Chro 16:9.[32]

Gid was feeling that tugging at his heart. "Gideon, now is the opportune time to inquire."

"Doctor, do you believe in God? Have you experienced his power in your life?"

Silence.

"Um, Reverend Gideon, this adoption is of great interest to me. I will want to know more about this, as time goes by."

"Reverend Gideon, when Dr. Lucas ordered Hospice for you, you had reached the stage in your disease process called End Stage CHF. You met the criteria for admission. I have written your care plan. You have received the support of our medical team, as well as received the durable medical equipment that is approved for your diagnosis.

---

[31] ((KJV) n.d.)
[32] ((NASB) n.d.)

"However, you are currently demonstrating improvement. This is unprecedented. Your admission is certified for six months. We will continue to follow you with visits throughout the certification period, then if improvement continues, we will discharge you back to your primary care physician. If you decline, you will be recertified for another six months. Reverend Gideon, you are a blessed man. I must admit, I am bewildered."

"Weak things confound the strong, Doc."

Almost stuttering, "Th-this is out of the ordinary. I look forward to our next visit. Reverend, good day."

Purah graciously showed him to the door, and as he left, he muttered, "This may just be 'terminal lucidity.' Time will tell."

#

Son of LaMar, Gid pondered.

Purah and Gid looked deeply into one another's face as if studying something unexplainable. "Baby," Gid said, "that man looks so familiar. My spirit certainly took notice. And Son of LaMar?"

Purah was feeling the emotion of the thought well up in her, with her eyes beginning to tear and feeling flushed. "Gid, that is exactly what I was thinking. Do we know him from somewhere? You may have seen him on a pastoral visit, while he saw one of his patients, but I would not have seen him."

CHAPTER FIFTEEN
LaMarah Calls

"Pansie, my skydiving lesson is in a few minutes." Ochre's heart was pounding. "Uh, just want you to know how much I love you—in case something happens."

"Oh, Ochre. Don't do me that way. I won't let you out of this house." She reluctantly closed the door.

Pansie grabbed the phone on the first ring just in case it was for Ochre. "Oh, LaMarah! Baby, let me catch your daddy."

"Ochre, Ochre! LaMarah is on the phone."

\#

Gid said, "Ochre is here with some exciting news, Purah."

Purah came out of the bedroom carrying Charity Grace. "Ochre, come in and sit down."

"Just give me a second. I don't know how much more excitement I can bear," she said.

Easing into the rocking chair, giving to the sharp pain in her back, Purah was thinking, "I need to stop dropping into chairs. I could fall with Charity Grace in my arms, then what would I do?"

"LaMarah called," Ochre said. "She said she has a layover and won't need to be back at Alexander until Monday. She will be coming by for a visit tomorrow."

Ochre was pondering his ups and downs. One minute he was planning a skydiving accident, the next he was excited about a visit.

"Why Ochre, that is the best news," said Purah.

"You know I am so proud of her," said Ochre. "Gid, but our relationship still suffers from her unplanned pregnancy, and the stand I took urging her to have an abortion."

"We will be so glad to see her, it has been years," said Gid.

Barely able to hold his coffee. "If I had known she would have married Mark later, I might have done a better job handling that situation."

Gid said, "So, how would marrying Mark have made a difference? Think about that, Ochre."

Considering, "All the while, her mother was urging me to let her have that baby. I really don't know how Pansie lived with me all these years.

"LaMarah just couldn't face me after the abortion and went away to college with our relationship completely broken.

"Everything was so convoluted. Mark took her for that abortion, and we have all suffered the aftermath. We have scarcely seen her since then. It's been thirty-five years! The heaviness in my heart turned from pain to bitterness.

"Every day, I have replayed those conversations, not effectively dealing with the aftermath. Oh, Gid, I know you know most of this, but I just need to talk.

"Gid, I am a mess."

"Ochre, do you think you have turned the bitterness inward?"

"Oh, yes, Gid, it is like a cancer eating on me all the time. Emotional garbage fills my life with not only depression, but anxiety, and even jealousy of others who are experiencing joy in their lives."

"One piece of advice that I have given many, Ochre, is study what scripture teaches about spiritual warfare. I don't have to tell you that your mind is a battlefield."

"Do I ever know that. There are times that I uh, I uh pray for God to forgive me for critical things, judgmental thi things I say and think about others. Gid, I so ne need to be able to resolve all this and let it go." The emotion was sapping Ochre's strength.

"Your battles will bring you victory soon."

"One overriding question is, why do I hurt people so deeply?"

"Ochre, God is accomplishing a great work right now. We are all a part of it. You know how God works. Knowing that healing waters are stirring can be a faith builder."

#

The next morning, Ochre's routine was to complete his one-mile walk. His mind was reeling with decades-old thoughts and questions. *How important is all that now? I know the pain for her was deep and she was so young to deal with that alone.*

Our pain of losing her was just as deep, but in a different way, he thought. *Our whole life revolved around her. Our hopes of her mending our schism never materialized. We tried many times to make amends, yet met barriers of busy with college, travel on breaks, and jobs far away. We realized the wound for her was too deep, she couldn't deal with it. So, we made advances with complete resistance.*

#

As Ochre's rigid body approached his front door, he saw a woman walking toward him. Frozen in time, his gaze was fixed on her purposeful gait and emotionless reaction to his presence.

She was wearing professional dress with beautiful long hair, parted, and braided around her face. "Daddy, is that you?"

She extended her hand to shake his.

"While straightening himself up, he said, "Oh, LaMarah baby, please let me hug you." By that time, they were both trembling. As they briefly hugged, Ochre said, "I am so sorry for all that happened."

She thought, *the years have not been good to him,* as she stared at his hands.

"Daddy," pulling away, "let's go inside."

Pansie was scurrying around making ready for LaMarah, and in they walked. "LaMarah, baby!" She could not hold back the tears. Weeping aloud, she fell on LaMarah's shoulder.

LaMarah began to soften. "Mama, I have missed you so much. I have needed you so many times. I just couldn't call. Something inside me would never let me do it. I have been so angry."

Pansie took her face in her hands and kissed her forehead. "Baby, I needed you too. I am so sorry. Can you ever forgive us?"

Skirting around the idea of forgiveness, LaMarah quickly said, "You did not know everything," while trying to regain her composure.

"You know I went away to college. You know that Mark and I later married.

"What you do not know is that I did not have the abortion. I gave birth to a beautiful baby boy."

Pansie said, "Oh, LaMarah! This makes me so happy!"

"I wanted so bad to keep him. With me in college, I didn't know what to do. I had no help. I placed him for adoption with a childless, middle-aged couple there in the college town. He was the pastor of the church where I attended."

"Do you ever see him?"

"They had agreed to let me see him one time a year around his birthday. I only observed him from a distance. I couldn't talk to him."

"Wh why didn't you tell us?" asked Ochre.

"Daddy, I felt like you had robbed me of my son. I could not come to grips with that. It took me years to realize that I had gone through a depression and was in a numb, disturbed existence. That is when I met back up with Mark. I knew he loved me; he believed we had a child together! He had been grieving as well. Soon, we married."

By this time, Pansie's grief was overwhelming her. Her voice was wailing. "Baby, I am so sorry you had to go through this alone."

"Mama, I know it was hard for you too. My grief progressed in steps."

"We have prayed every day for you. We have prayed for guidance, for wisdom, and for God to just help us cope with this," said Pansie.

"There were times I would slip backward two steps, then inch back forward. I really began to realize how hard it was for you after I had my second child.

"I harbored the bitterness for so long, it was like a cancer. Mark tried to get me to forgive you, so that I could go on with my life.

"It affected my health, and it affected my relationship with my children. I had seasons of depression where I couldn't sleep or eat. All I wanted to do was sleep and couldn't do that.

"It continued to gnaw on me. I was thinking about dying and death, so when Mark learned that he made me seek therapy. It wasn't hard to get to the cause, but I realized through counseling I was also ashamed of placing my baby for adoption. When I began to deal with that, I began to get better.

"I am so glad that I had a Christian counselor. He helped me to point out the things that I am thankful for.

"Mama, Daddy, I am thankful for the upbringing that you gave me.

"I am thankful for being raised in this remarkable town. You don't know this, but I have kept up with everything going on in Harbor Oaks. I get the local *Lighthouse News and Views* each week. I see all the births and marriages. I see all the politics and sports, as well as who visits who in the Society section. I guess that helped me in a counterfeit kind of way. My heart is always here, though."

"I am so glad, LaMarah, that you gave birth to your baby. I can't tell you how much peace that gives me." Pansie dared mention that this separation had affected her health too. She had suffered with severe Crohns with many surgeries and complications.

"So, what caused you to not abort the baby?"

"I am afraid that may be a topic for another day. I want to visit with all the Oaks while I am here. I have read that Chef Nathaniel is awesome. Let's go over and be sociable. Isn't it about time for dinner?"

"We have some time yet. Let's walk down to the Harbor Oaks River Park," said Pansie.

Ochre had been mostly silent through the conversation but opened once they got to the Park.

"LaMarah, I feel like a huge burden was lifted off my chest. Not only am I glad we can reconcile, but I am pleased and thankful that you did not abort the baby.

"Since those days, I have done a lot of soul searching, and I believe we are in a constant warfare with Satan." Turning stiffly toward her, "I have repeatedly asked myself, how I could have allowed that to happen?

"Reverend Gideon frequently reminds us, 'Satan's goal is to destroy the Christian and their testimony.'

"Baby, let's sit here near these whitewashed oaks."

LaMarah said, "He certainly attacked our family and came close to giving us the 'death blow.'"

"I now realize Satan's desire is to destroy Christians, either by destroying our influence and testimony or to destroy our health, to keep us from accomplishing God's plan for our lives. Knowing this helped me see what is going on in the spiritual realm regarding our family," said Ochre.

"Dad, spiritual warfare uses our mind for the battlefield."

"Oh, LaMarah, that is the same thing Gid was talking about."

"That's right," she said. "We must learn to take every thought captive by tearing down strongholds that Satan will create in our minds. I can see myself putting both hands on those thoughts and throwing them to the ground, checking them for untruth the enemy has planted.

"We cannot receive the negative thoughts that Satan offers. We must learn to recognize his lies and refuse giving them a place to germinate and grow."

"So that is what Gid was referring to as weapons of warfare," said Ochre.

"Daddy, why would we feed those lies with agreement? Why would we give those lies a place to hurt others?"

"LaMarah, at my age, I am still learning. I have learned that I have allowed Satan to use me. Even though I am a Christian, I have not kept my mind filled with God's Word. I have failed to refuse thoughts that would come close to destroying me and my family. I have been a weak warrior."

"Daddy, Mama, let's set some goals for healing."

Ochre began, "My goal now is to use those weapons God gave me to win the battles. I am going to allow the Holy Spirit to guard my mind. For me to do it, I must stay in the Word daily.

"I believe that is why God is allowing us to reconcile. I am allowing the Holy Spirit to tear down those strongholds Satan built in my mind. Those thoughts would feed my ego, and my pride.

"I was putting my success before my relationship with God. I failed to thank Him for my attainments, my abilities, recognitions, and status.

"Although, I knew I could not have done those things without God's favor, I did not recognize Him, as I should. You know, I had such an humble beginning. I was just a little barefoot plow boy. I should have been willing to acknowledge God as the giver of those gifts. So many things had to happen for me to get through high school, much less college. Then marrying Pansie gave our life an anchor. Her faith was our mooring. I now realize that I depended on her faith and not mine."

"Mama, do you have a goal?"

"Baby, my goal is to ask God to change my attitude. I have had very destructive thoughts. At times I have wanted to end my life."

Ochre reached for her hand and looked at the floor.

"I have been passive aggressive with your dad. Blaming him in a lefthanded kind of way enabled me to stuff my anger and grief. Ochre, please forgive me. I know that was destructive to our relationship."

LaMarah said, "My goal is complete reconciliation. Mark and our sons need to be a part of this."

"Oh, Daddy, bitterness is so destructive. It leaves a path of devastation and ruin. I too am an example of that. What is the cure for bitterness?"

Pansie replied, "If that is our prayer, God will show us."

"LaMarah," said Pansie, "our Oaks—Gid calls us the Oaks now—are praying to be able to share our talents and our experiences in a meaningful way. Even though we are showing signs of aging, God endowed us with a wealth of abilities we believe He is about to use for His glory. Right here under this grove of Oaks, God revealed to Reverend Gideon imminent plans for our *Closing Life-Challenge*. I want him to share that with you."

"Daddy, the reverend's friendship is something I have cherished all these years. Who can ever put a value on a friendship?"

Taking a deep breath, feeling liberated, LaMarah studied her dad's face, seeing the tremors in his hands. "You are struggling to walk, Dad. What is going on?" Not knowing when she would see him again, she felt liberty to inquire about his health.

"LaMarah, I do not know. I need to see a doctor soon. We have so much going on with the Gideons' failing health and the adoption, it preoccupies all of us."

"What is going on, Dad?"

"No way to shorten this long story, LaMarah. Gid's failing health is our major concern. There is much more to this. I will let them tell you about it.

"We have a celebration planned for you tomorrow after church in the park. Our Chef Nat, here at the AL Community, is catering our lunch."

CHAPTER SIXTEEN
The Cure for Bitterness

Grace Is the Forgiveness Key

The Oaks were gathering in the chapel for worship. The repurposed ship bell, *Charity Grace*, began to slowly rock, then swing, then loudly toll.

LaMarah was startled. "What *is* that?"

David had prepared an arrangement of "Savior Like a Shepherd Lead Us,"[33] for the Call to Worship. Stepping across the threshold, Reverend Gideon along with the choir began a slow two-step processional, then finding their designated places.

David gave the downbeat.

As LaMarah slipped into the pew, her senses were heightened to the simple beauty surrounding her. "Too many years have passed, from the time I found myself on my knees in a worship setting, Mama."

The time with her dad had unlocked the numbness she had cloaked in her grief.

---

[33] (Martin n.d.)

LaMarah, now weeping, whispered to her mom, "Hearing the choir with that magnificent harmony is mesmerizing. I have missed the worship here at Harbor Oaks more than I realized."

With reverence and pride, Reverend Gideon stood and proceeded to take his position behind the pulpit.

#

"We, my friends, are the 'Oaks' spoken of in the scripture read, *that* day.

"The scripture on *that* day is actualized in my life.

"My doctor said I am making remarkable improvement on *this* day.

"On *that* day, this old warrior was given a new battle. A different kind of war. We know our warfare is not with flesh and blood.

"A war not with people as enemies, but this, my dear *Oaks*, is a war with precedent. This precedent is an accepted standard, a standard with no authority.

"That precedent says a 'weak person is unable to achieve'. That precedent says, 'a weak person cannot succeed'.

"That precedent stood, unchallenged. Today, by the grace of God, I challenge that precedent! I challenge that precedent that has *no* authority.

"The authority in my life is the Holy Spirit of God.

He has said to me, today, as he said to the apostle Paul:"

My grace is sufficient for thee: for my strength is made perfect in weakness. Most gladly therefore will I rather glory in my infirmities, that the power of Christ may rest upon me. Therefore, I take pleasure in infirmities, in reproaches, in necessities, in persecutions, in distresses for Christ's sake: for when I am weak, then am I strong. 2 Cor. 12:9-10.[34]

#

"Brothers and sisters, friends, I am honored to stand before you *this* day.

"Brothers and sisters, tonight, I will be speaking on 'The Cure for Bitterness.'

"Jesus himself breathed the Holy Spirit on His weak disciples just before he ascended to the Father.

"Purah, will you read the scripture for *this* day? Blessed be the reading of the word."

Then the same day at evening, being the first day of the week, when the doors were shut where the disciples were assembled for fear of the Jews, came Jesus and stood in the midst, and saith unto them, Peace be unto you.

And when he had so said, he shewed unto them his hands and his side. Then were the disciples glad, when they saw the Lord (John 20:19-20).[35]

"Yeeesireee," said Miller.

"Well, well, well," said Dr. Morrison. Then he doubled both fists, saying, "That's my Jesus. Ah yes, Peace."

---

[34] ((KJV) n.d.)
[35] ((KJV) n.d.)

Gid's spirit was visibly stirred. "Peace be unto you, as the Father has sent Me, I also send you. I also send you!" v.21.[36] Then pausing, and lifting his voice, "Oaks," he said, 'I also send you!'

"Then v. 22-23,

"And when he had said this, he breathed on them, and saith unto them, Receive ye the Holy Ghost: Whosoever sins ye remit, they are remitted unto them; and whosoever sins ye retain, they are retained.[37]

Pansie gave a hearty "amen," sitting there with hands raised, head bowed, weeping.

"The disciples most certainly felt weak, after their experience with Jesus' betrayal, arrest, trial, suffering, and crucifixion. There was nothing the disciples were able to do to stop that brutal process.

"But then, something was added to the problem. Something that would change the equation forever was added to their weakness and faith. That something was His Resurrection. Brothers, sisters, with the Resurrection came the indwelling of the Holy Spirit in every believer.

"The Holy Spirit empowered them to activate the gifts God had given them to minister, even in their weakness. It wasn't a problem at all. They just didn't have all the factors. But now, their minds were doing flips. He just breathed the Holy Spirit onto them."

Miller waived his crooked arm. "That's my God!"

"Their old system required an animal sacrifice in order to be forgiven of sin, and that had to be done every year. Now, by the Holy Spirit, they could be instruments of forgiveness, because of Jesus' perfect blood sacrifice given once and given for all.

---

[36] ((KJV) n.d.)
[37] (Ibid n.d.)

"I ask you, Oaks, what part do we play in forgiveness? Ask yourselves, 'What part do *I* play in forgiveness?'"

After a grand pause, he continued.

"I am talking to those of us Oaks who are blessed because:

1. Our roots are by the stream.
2. We are planted beside and watered by the river of life.
3. We have no fear of heat.
4. We have no worries of drought.
5. We never fail to bear fruit. Never fail! Never!"

In their excitement, with raised hands, the Oaks rose to their feet, shouting, "Never fail! Never! Never!"

Gid stepped back from the pulpit and gave another pause.

As the Oaks' loud and animated agreements subsided, Gid once again stepped forward and took hold of the Horns of the Altar.

"Yes, beloved we pray for the Holy Spirit to empower us, the Church, His body.

"These people who just months earlier had seen Jesus, had heard Him teach, and saw Him as he was dying on the cross, saying:

"'Father, forgive them; for they know not what they do.' Luke23:34a.[38]

"That, my beloved friends, is Power. It takes Authority to forgive sin. The Crucifixion of Jesus was all a part of God's plan. He permitted it. Jesus freely gave His life in order that we could have that forgiveness.

---

[38] ((KJV) n.d.)

"At Stephen's martyrdom, Acts 7:60b, he was being stoned, and his dying words were: 'Lord, lay not this sin to their charge. And when he had said this, he fell asleep.'[39]

"What a testimony to the love and grace of God. In Stephen's death, he was teaching his most powerful sermon. People who knew the truth (were looking for and had seen their Messiah and crucified him) were experiencing forgiveness. Stephen had the power to forgive those who sinned against him. They didn't deserve forgiveness.

"What if Stephen had not prayed that prayer?

"What if Saul had not heard Stephen pray for him to be forgiven?

"Acts 8:1a: and Saul was consenting unto his (Stephen's) death.[40]

"I ask you, 'who was Saul?' My beloved Oaks, are you with me?

"I ask you, 'who was Paul?'

"God used Paul in such powerful ways despite his claim to have been the 'chief of sinners.' (I Tim 1:15)[41]

"1Timothy 1:13-14, Who was before a blasphemer, and a persecutor, and injurious: but I obtained mercy, because I did it ignorantly in unbelief. And the grace of our Lord was exceeding abundant with faith and love which is in Christ Jesus."[42]

"Paul himself later prayed in II Tim 4:16b, 'but all men forsook me: I pray God that it may not be laid to their charge.'[43]

"What do we want to see the Holy Spirit do in our lives?

---

[39] ((KJV) n.d.)
[40] ((KJV) n.d.)
[41] ((KJV) n.d.)
[42] (Ibid n.d.)
[43] ((KJV) n.d.)

"Peter expressed his faith in the 'Christ,' and listen to what Christ told him."

And I say also unto thee, That thou art Peter, and upon this rock I will build my church; and the gates of hell shall not prevail against it. And I will give unto thee the keys of the kingdom of heaven: and whatsoever thou shalt bind on earth shall be bound in heaven: and whatsoever thou shalt loose on earth shall be loosed in heaven. Matt 16:18-19[44]

"Beloved, those keys are what opens the gates of the kingdom of heaven. Grace is the forgiveness key. Grace is a gift. Grace is undeserved. So, the gates of heaven are open, and the gates of hell shall not prevail!

"So, are we binding forgiveness on earth? Forgiveness will lose the bonds of sin. Forgiving others will set us free, not because the person forgiven deserves it, but because Jesus paid *our* sin debt. Jesus Christ suffered, freely gave his life on that cruel cross, and rose from the dead to appropriate our forgiveness. His is forgiveness that gives us eternal life.

"We have authority to share that powerful salvation story through the Holy Spirit that Jesus breathed on the disciples on that day, announcing that belief in what Jesus wrought at calvary will yield forgiveness and that the gates of heaven are open.

"The Lord says a lot about forgiveness.

"Luke 6:37: 'Forgive, and ye shall be forgiven.'[45] And in Matthew 6:15: 'But if ye forgive not men their trespasses, neither will your

---

[44] ((KJV) n.d.)
[45] ((KJV) n.d.)

Father forgive your trespasses.[46] Now…I ask, *Oaks*, what part do we play in forgiveness?

"Do we pray for the Holy Spirit to empower us, to empower the church?

"I implore you, what do we want to see the Holy Spirit do?

"John 14:12: 'Verily, verily, I say unto you, He that believeth on me, the works that I do shall he do also; and greater works than these shall he do; because I go unto my Father.'[47]

"What greater works than healing the sick can we do? They had witnessed him healing the sick—then he gave them the new commandment to *love one another*, and then 'greater works.'"

"Oaks, Church, what will it be? Grace or grief?

"We can kick our brothers who fail to the curb, or we can forgive them and see the power of the Holy Spirit strengthen the body of Christ. He will give us Beauty for Ashes.

To appoint unto them that mourn in Zion, to give unto them beauty for ashes, the oil of joy for mourning, the garment of praise for the spirit of heaviness; that they might be called trees of righteousness, the planting of the Lord, that he might be glorified, Isaiah 61:3.[48]

"Trees of righteousness, I leave you with one thought. Forgiveness is the cure for bitterness, that Christ may be glorified, in us, the believer."

Stepping aside, "Anyone here feel the need to share?"

Ochre, holding the pew for support with his left hand, and in a victory wave from his shaking right hand, started to vigorously shout,

---

[46] ((KJV) n.d.)
[47] ((KJV) n.d.)
[48] ((KJV) n.d.)

"This day, I have forgiven my father for neglecting me as a child, after my mother died. I used my bitterness as a guide for my whole life to enable me to be harsh and cold.

"My teacher, Mr. Weeks, was a friend to our family and did what he could to lead me into wholesome activity. He would pick me up for ball practice, helped me get my Eagle Scout badge, and even took me to church. His encouragement kept this youngster busy and mostly out of trouble.

"Oh, but I still had an emptiness in my heart and never forgave my dad. My adult life was an example of someone who became very legalistic without allowing love to temper my interaction with others. Why, I even prided myself with expecting others to meet my heartless standards.

"Pansie, you have been more than an angel. How have you lived with me all these years? Your inner constitution enabled you to hear my rantings and hold your tongue. How did you do it? I ask you right now, if you can find it in your heart, can you please forgive me?

"LaMarah, baby, you have been the one to suffer the most. You, my precious little girl. I alienated you for all these years. I know the resentment and bitterness in your heart almost destroyed you. I know that I do not deserve forgiveness, but I beg you, please forgive me?"

LaMarah rose from the pew, reaching for him, "Oh, Daddy, I have forgiven you. Coming here was my first step. I am laying that burden on Jesus, never to pick it up again.

"Finally, though, I came close to destroying myself," she said.

Ochre covered his face and sobbed. "Some things can't be fixed." Crumpling into a heap on the pew he said, "How, Reverend Gideon, can we be restored? How can we go forward?"

Holding up his Bible in his right hand, "Ochre, you are an Oak. I want you to realize that God is giving you what you need to move forward. He is giving us all what we need." With more intensity, "We are all weak. Paul said, 'when I am weak, then I am strong.' 2 Cor 12:10.[49] We have all drank the dregs of sin. Jesus took up the gauntlet for us, and He drank."

Then laying his Bible on the pulpit, raising both hands as if holding on to God, "He is standing ready to lead us onto this battlefield. Yes, we are a weak army, but we have the Captain of God's Angel Army to lead us to victory. God doesn't need our strength or our weapons. He needs our faith, then our belief that births obedience.

"Forgiveness is the cure for bitterness. Ochre, you have forgiven those who wronged you. You have asked forgiveness from those you wronged. Your bitterness is cured. You are healed.

"Psalm 107:19-20 says: 'Then they cry unto the LORD in their trouble, and he saveth them out of their distresses. He sent his word, and healed them, and delivered them from their destructions.'"[50]

After a few moments of wiping tears Ochre stood and said, "Forgiveness washes it away."

Reverend Gideon said, "Let us adjourn to the Harbor Oaks River Park, where Chef Nathaniel is setting up a wonderful lunch, he's planned for us. We have so much to celebrate."

#

Making their way to the park, LaMarah asked her mother, "Whatever possessed you and Dad to name me LaMarah? Knowing all my life that my name meant bitter—plagues me."

"Oh, LaMarah. We were the ones who were bitter. We were coming out of the Great Depression when you were born. I had lost

---

[49] ((KJV) n.d.)
[50] ((KJV) n.d.)

Daddy in a logging accident. Mama kept his bloody clothes in a trunk until she died. Our family needed him so badly.

"Your daddy didn't have a job, and there I was having a baby."

"Why didn't you tell me all this?"

"Honey, you knew most of it. You just didn't know the depth of emotion we were experiencing at the time.

"We all went hungry to pay the bills. I just couldn't see how we would be able to afford another mouth to feed. Mother's sister over in the next town kept you for us for several months while I looked for a job and tried to earn some money to bring you home.

"I was bitter with God. 'LaMarah' was pretty enough name, but it was my complaint with God. Why did we have such hardship? We had dreams of a better life. You were the best thing that could have ever happened. We just had too much on our plate to value that part of our life.

"Ochre was still going to his 'Crazy Granny's' cabin every day to be where his mother died. You were several years old, before Ochre finished his education."

"Mom, it all makes sense. I suppose there are many talks we could have had, if I had been around. We must make the most of our time together. Can you forgive me for not being here?"

CHAPTER SEVENTEEN
Crew to Oaks

LaMarah, arriving in the park, was eager to renew friendships with the Oaks. She asked Miller, "What happened to change your name from the Crew to the Oaks?"

"It was Gid's teaching that nailed it for us all. We had all been praying about what to do with all the experience and talent we possess. I guess it was a kind of grief over our losses, which we were trying to process. We talked of it frequently, without any direction."

"God spoke to Gid, right here in the park one rainy evening. He told him something very decisive. I am thinking it would be best for him to tell you this, since he is here."

"Gid, what is all the mystery about this name change, the adoption, and your *Closing Life-Challenge*?"

"LaMarah, the short of it is, we are adopting a baby. To begin to tell this makes my head spin, when I think of all that is transpiring during this process."

LaMarah's head cocked back. She raised her eyebrows and had a half grin. "*You* are adopting a baby?"

"To begin, my health had declined to the point that Dr. Lucas had put me on Hospice."

"Oh, Gid, no!"

"I said 'had.' our Oaks had been praying almost to the point of wrestling with God, about what we could do to share our talents and experiences. Our minds are all still sharp, although we are advanced in age and our bodies are wearing out."

"After talking with Dr. Lucas that Wednesday afternoon, I managed to maneuver myself here to the park. The wind was kicking up, and I knew it was about to rain. However, I needed to talk to God and get direction on the scripture for our prayer meeting. There I was in a daze from the news of my diagnosis. Physically struggling with my congestive heart failure, I could hardly pick up my feet to inch along, much less breathe with the extra exertion of walking.

"The Lord visited me here that day. He told me I had been a 'Valiant Warrior.' He reminded me how he uses us in our weakest state. I walked home in the pouring rain and when I walked into the house, there was not a wet thread on my body. Most of the Oaks were there and commented about it.

"That evening, I spoke on Psalm 1:3 and Jer. 17:5 'They shall be like a Tree planted by the water.'[51] God was in our midst. There was such movement of the Holy Spirit in that room. Praises and shouting were common throughout the service. I shared with them the things the Lord told me in the grove.

"Then, a couple of days later, one of our attendants had given birth to a baby girl and left her here with Purah and me. We learned a few days later that the Mom had died. We found a will that she left concerning the baby. She wanted us to take responsibility for her. LaMarah, we all knew this was the *Closing Life-Challenge* that God wanted us to undertake.

---

[51] ((KJV) n.d.)

"God is moving in our presence. That is what I got from the song on *that* night."

"Oh, I am beginning to see. So, the Oaks came from the scripture. And, what about your health, Gid?"

"My condition is improved to the point where the Hospice doctor is considering taking me off Hospice and referring me back to my primary care physician, Dr. Lucas."

"So, do you believe your improvement is related to the *Closing Life-Challenge*?"

"LaMarah, I have no doubt. I feel like a fifty-year-old man."

"How do the others play into this?"

"LaMarah, each one is taking responsibility to teach her the talents they have. It already is amazing how much she is learning. DFS was planning to place her with someone for permanent adoption. Charity Grace's condition noticeably declined. The pediatrician diagnosed her with 'failure to thrive.' We were able to get the judge to place her back with us, at least temporarily. This is part of the battle, but we are hoping they will find her father, and he will honor the mother's wishes."

"So, LaMarah, we the Oaks are in a Parenting Paradox battle. I am sure this will make the paper. When you read about it, just know God is in control." "Gid, I am leaving town, and wonder if it will be okay to let my parents know the details of what happened thirty-five years ago?"

"LaMarah, that is your call."

CHAPTER EIGHTEEN
LaMarah's Confession

Nathaniel served up the most wonderful fried catfish that lips had ever caressed. Knowing what the Oaks grew up on made him the ideal Harbor Oaks soul chef. The collards with pot liquor and cheese grits were among his most sought-after recipes, not to mention his hushpuppy recipe with onion and corn.

LaMarah went from person to person hugging and kissing them, feeling that she may never see them again.

Years had accumulated since they were all together. LaMarah had not aged well—credited with the depression and anxiety from years of bitterness.

As the celebration was ending, she calmly asked for their attention. "My sweet friends, I love you more than you can know. The *Lighthouse News and Views* newspaper is always on my kitchen table, so I know what goes on in Harbor Oaks, but I realize there is little that you all know about me and my family."

"When I left Harbor Oaks, I was pregnant, out of wedlock." LaMarah was surprised that she didn't hear any gasps. "My parents and I had scheduled an abortion."

She pondered: *This group of people never seemed to pass judgment on others*. Looking around, she saw the love in each tear-filled eye, which she had often talked about as she grew up in Harbor Oaks. *How I adored the stories they told of their beloved teacher friend, Mr. Weeks, about how he endowed in them the awareness that 'it is not our job to judge others.' He took teamwork to a whole new level.*

"Not only was I so stricken with grief," she said, "I was conflicted about taking the life of my unborn baby to cover up my mistake. I sought counsel from Reverend Gideon, and he urged me not to go through with it. He told me he would do whatever necessary to save my baby's life. I was so confused. This was the worst thing ever to happen to me and I was not equipped to handle it.

"We scheduled the abortion. Mark planned on taking me. When we arrived, I was beside myself. Mark and I fought all the way to the abortion clinic, and I told him to leave me there. I would call Daddy to pick me up. I called Reverend Gideon."

"Gid laughed. "Excuse me for laughing but I tore out of a wedding reception when Purah called me. I didn't anymore get onto the main road when I got stopped for speeding. I wasn't making much sense to the officer, and he was about to arrest me for being under the influence. He finally understood me and gave me an escort all the way to the abortion clinic. I brought LaMarah home, and her parents didn't know she didn't have the abortion. Mark didn't know."

LaMarah continued, "That's right, I didn't tell Mom and Daddy. I went on to college that fall and closed the door on them. I wouldn't talk to them or visit. I always had excuses, but they never knew that I had given birth to a beautiful baby boy. They also didn't know; his father was a thirteen-year-old who had a crush on me."

Taking a deep breath, "The months that followed were pure torment for me." Pacing in front of the group, "I imagined every scenario that would enable me to keep my baby. I loved him so much. How could I raise a child and me with no education? I know it is done, but my mind was showing me all the dangers for an unwed mother, the potential of having him taken away by DFS, and what's more I had no resources."

It was obvious, relating this story was exceedingly difficult for her.

"To shorten a long story, I placed him for adoption. All I know about him is he is a doctor. I never see him.

"Mark and I later married. We have two sons. They bring us so much joy. We have had many difficulties because of the unplanned pregnancy and the way I handled it. Daddy, Mama, I am so deeply sorry for the way I handled it. I forgive you both. I hope you can forgive me."

"Learning about Spiritual Warfare and how to pray gives me so much understanding. I grew up in church but having a pregnancy out of wedlock was not in my plans. Once I cut myself off from the two people in the world who loved me most, I didn't have what I needed emotionally or spiritually to make the right decisions. I am thankful for one thing, that I gave birth.

"Thank you, Reverend Gideon and Purah, for the good counsel you gave me and for the support afterward." LaMarah embraced them both and wept for what seemed like a lengthy time.

"LaMarah, we felt like it was the only thing to do. Our spirit has been with you, through all these years," said Purah.

LaMarah heard Purah whisper to her in a soft voice, "In Christ alone."

Purah and Gid's love drew LaMarah deep into their souls. *Their foundation is unshakeable,* she thought. *How or what or who would bring people to such a giving spirit, such a grace-filled life?* Her heart felt as though it was moving within her. "The two of you are what living is all about."

Feeling empowered, "I must be leaving. I am to be back at work in the morning. We are going to keep in touch. Goodbye I love you all, with my whole heart."

"Mark was so right," she said. "I do feel so free."

As Gid and Purah watched her leave, Purah commented, "Her baby boy is a doctor, Gid."

CHAPTER NINETEEN
Teacher Weeks Passed the Baton

Gid mused, we were taught by the "Good Book" to love others, to "keep ourselves in the love of God."

"Purah, I think often about Mr. Weeks, how he poured himself into our lives. That man loved us and believed in us. He was a shepherd, keeping his eye out for the wolves in our lives. The wolves that would devour us, whether it was a bad personal decision like selfishness or failing to plan for our own future.

"I remember how us boys liked to fight. It didn't take anything to start it. One day Hughey came inside after recess with a bloody nose, his red hair in a knotted mess, and dust all over his arms and pants. Mr. Weeks kind of chuckled. 'Hughey, who have you been fighting with this time? I believe you would fight with Lucifer. I guess you know, I am going to have to punish you. You are going to have to stay in during play period.'

"Hughey said, 'He called me Red, Mr. Weeks. Mr. Weeks, who is Lucifer?' The kids all rolled with laughter and Mr. Weeks said, 'Hughey, you go get the mop and oil bucket. Mop this floor. Hughey, you've got a good memory, but it's short. Do you think you can remember to solve your problem a better way, next time?'

Fighting was boys favored past time.

"There he was, giving poor Hughey a compliment in the middle of his punishment. We all loved him and Mrs. Weeks.[52]"

"Yes, I remember," said Purah.

"We were so impressionable," said Gid.

Purah said, "I never knew anyone who went to college, before I was in middle school. In those days, teachers weren't required to have college. Mr. Weeks told us he wanted to go to college so bad, he walked and hitchhiked from Ellijay to Berry College, in Rome, Georgia. Mr. Weeks would talk about living in the dorm at Berry College. In their day, there wasn't any electricity in the dorm rooms. All they had was coal fireplaces and oil lamps for light. He said, 'In the winter, we would keep our milk outside the window on the ledge to keep it cold.'

"I could imagine," said Purah. "Even in my day, we didn't have electricity. I believe his stories were meant to show us that we could do anything if we just tried, if we just would not give up."

Gid said, "Picking us up and taking us to church was just one of the many things they did. They never showed any difference in the other 'boys and girls,' and me. I was one of the only black children in the classroom. I may have looked different, but he demonstrated daily that our hearts were all the same to God. He made sure we all knew he loved us, and that God loved us.

"Our history classes were the most interesting. As we sat in those little desks, you would have believed he fought in those battles giving detailed descriptions, waving his arms, yelling commands to the flanks of soldiers, and where they were entrenched, engaging in battle. He read weekly history articles from the *CJC*, describing field hospitals, hungry barefoot soldiers without adequate rations and training, and the families they left behind. Then there were the stories of the heroes of

---

[52] (Etta Mae Dunn Weeks May 14, 1908-March 21, 1998)

141

the underground railroad. There was always a noble lesson to learn of perseverance, frugality, brotherly love, or wit and wisdom within the ranks.

"He took time every day while we waited for the last bell to give us good advice.

"'Boys and girls buy you some land and plant some loblolly pines. They don't take much care over the years and you will have money for your retirement. You will know when they are ready to harvest because the tops will no longer be pointed but will look flat.' He was investing in us, day by day, lesson by lesson. Those investments paid great dividends to us boys and girls. I'm guessing that is what is meant by 'paying it forward.' What an example he demonstrated for us. He lived it out.

"We all did that very thing. Our daddies were all sharecroppers. We didn't have anything of our own, and land was cheap—about twenty dollars[53] an acre. We all bought a little land and planted loblolly pines. He told us to. We all retired without worry.

"That man made a difference in the lives of us boys and girls. We had confidence that we could do anything we tried. We had been taught faith in our creator God, respect for our elders, love for our country, and we were taught that 'a man shouldn't eat if he doesn't work.'

"After all these years, I still think back to those days. I can still hear him say, 'Don't ever date anybody you wouldn't want to marry.' At that time, I had not even thought about dating. I can't help but wonder where we all would be had it not been for Mr. Weeks.

---

[53]   (http://usda.mannlib.cornell.edu/usda/AgCensusImages/1940/01/28/1264/Table-02.pdf n.d.)

"You know, Mr. Weeks was part of God's plan for our lives. The things he passed to us we have passed along to others. And now, rightly so, to Charity Grace."

"You mean, that was his legacy, Gid?"

"Exactly. I sure hope we have been diligent to do the things we were taught, and not only do them, but to teach others to do them, Purah. Yes, he passed to us the baton."

"Oh, Baby, you have been faithful to all he taught you and more," said Purah. "He prepared you for the adversity you faced in the social change through these decades. Your parents weren't equipped for those battles. You went on to follow your calling in ministry and have been a catalyst for change here in Zion Baptist Church and the community. Gid, your steadfastness makes a difference. You *are* the 'Valiant Warrior' the Lord called there on the riverbank on *that* day."

"Baby, I feel like a wet dishrag when it comes to being used by the Lord. I am glad I learned He knows what He is doing. That sure gives me a lot of peace. If I thought for a minute the results of this *Closing Life-Challenge* were up to me, I would not have taken up the gauntlet. There are plenty of valid reasons to sit this one out. My prayer is: we will be able to effectively teach Charity Grace to love her fellow man as Christ loves us. If we do, we will be the Oaks He destined us to be."

"Gid, that is my hope and that we will be able to make a difference in her father, as well."

"That gauntlet may have some bitter dregs, but I believe we are able to use our spiritual weapons of warfare to tear down the objectionable strongholds."

CHAPTER TWENTY
LaMarah's Baby Is a Hospice Doctor

"Gid, that little stinker is scooting all over her bed. Do you think she is about to crawl? Maybe we are overstimulating her." Gid reached for her as she was reaching for his nose.

"Purah, I believe she would fret or cry if that were the case.

"Isn't that right, Charity Grace? You are my smart little girl. You are just looking for attention."

"I believe they call that spoiling, Gid."

"I would rather think of it as loving, Purah. If she is overstimulated, it is from all the love she is trying to adjust to. Many children grow up loved, but her two parents who are with her continuously, then with all the Oaks parenting her moment by moment, just maybe she is overstimulated. She indeed is learning quickly.

"If I didn't know this was God's plan, I would worry about her future and losing each of us to death, while she is so young. God is in control, and we need not give that a thought, but I believe it will come up in court, during the adoption process."

"Gid, Dr. Solomon is coming up the walk.

"Come in, Doctor. You got here just in time to see Gid making a fool of himself with Charity Grace. He is in another world with her."

"Come in, Doc," Gid said. "Make yourself comfortable. Can we get you something to drink?"

Doc was a short, trim man with thick wavy black hair a mesmerizing smile and brown eyes.

A noble face thought Gid.

"Doc, I must have met your acquaintance sometime in the past. You are so familiar."

"Reverend Gideon, I don't recall ever having met you."

Motioning to Purah, Gid said, "I want you to try Nathaniel's peanut butter pie. Purah will bring you a piece. You know Nathaniel put on a big spread for us Oaks, yesterday out at the Harbor Oaks Park. Ochre's daughter, LaMarah, popped in for a short visit."

"LaMarah, huh. That is a unique name. I haven't heard it often. That is my mother's name."

"So, you know you mother's name, Doc?"

Somewhat uncomfortable, "I don't know her. I just have some detail about my adoption."

"I can imagine, it must make you feel very blessed to have been adopted. Were you an infant?"

"I have limited facts, but I know my mother was a college student at the time. I don't know anything about my father."

"Listen, Doc, I can tell you from my experience in counseling women with unplanned pregnancies, when placing their baby for adoption, they are torn. Without a doubt, they love their baby, Doc. It is a sacrificial love. They want so badly to keep the baby; however, they sense their inability and resources. They forego their own desire and rights to give the baby what they hope is a better life."

"Reverend Gideon, I must admit, I have a lot of questions regarding my adoption. I love my parents, but I feel that I am not a whole person. Sacrificial love, huh?"

"You may never know all the facts, Doc, but you can know God's plan for your life. I am sure you already see that His hand is on you."

"Doc, if you know who your birth parents are, what difference will that make to you?" asked Purah.

"That is something I have thought a lot about." Looking into the distance, "I realize they may not want me in their lives. Just being placed for adoption causes me to feel a certain rejection." Walking over to the window, looking down to the whitewashed oaks, "I must be prepared for more rejection. I waited until I got out of medical school to deal with this. It is a heavy burden and adding that to my studies would have been inadvisable."

"Is that a step you are going to pursue?"

"Probably. I have taken a small step. What I know now is, my mother lives in Nashville."

"What is your next step?"

Turning again to the window, visibly stirred, "I believe my next step is to find out what I can about her family life, etc."

"My observation and advice here, you are about to make a judgment call on whether she would want to meet you. That is not your decision. That is hers. Give her the option," said Gid.

"You have such remarkable incite, and shall I say boldness?"

"Doc, my frankness is something I have learned from life experience. It is not judgmental—it is deep, compassionate honesty. Ben, son, our encounter is not of our making." Gid refrained from showing his hand.

"I don't know when I will see you again, if ever. You have begun making strides toward this victory in your life. It is within your reach," said Gid. "Please let me know about your progress, Doc."

Feeling a little embarrassed, "Reverend, I believe you have put this in proper perspective for me. I will keep you abreast."

After the examination, "Reverend Gideon, my conclusion today is that you are not in end-stage CHF. Based on that diagnosis, I am discharging you from Hospice. Our office will make you a follow-up appointment with Dr. Lucas, next week. Nurse Cathy will come by later today to finalize the paperwork.

"Reverend Gideon, this does not happen every day. My best, to you and Mrs. Gideon, and Charity Grace.

"Mrs. Gideon, I must be going."

Handing the ball cap to him, Purah said, "Doc, God's speed to you. I feel we will be seeing you again in a much different scenario."

"Ms. Purah, Reverend Gideon, if I can do anything to help expedite this *Closing Life-Challenge*, please give me the honor."

Nodding to them both, "Goodbye."

#

"That was interesting, Gid. What do you think he will do?"

"Baby, he knows. He is already attempting to identify with his mother. Did you see that ball cap? 'The Admirals.' His decision was not who, but what."

"Charity Grace, it sure was hard for me to keep my mouth shut while Doc was here. Don't you think I did a rather awesome job?" said Purah.

CHAPTER TWENTY-ONE
Live encounter news

The buzz was all over the Live Encounter news station. The old folks at Harbor Oaks Assisted Living had adopted a baby. The station manager was looking over the bullets for tonight's news.

Chuck was thinking, *I've got to get that interview. Let me see what Marketing is doing about those proposed trails.*

The producer said, "The construction is imminent."

Chuck asked, "Will there be a press release?"

"Yes, Chuck, we are planning a day to announce it and to mark it with a celebration."

"That would be a great time to get interviews," Chuck injected. "Party time always loosens lips."

"Sorry, Chuck, you may need to find a different avenue. These folks don't imbibe."

"Okay, I don't know if I have ever partied with old folks. What do you do? This is a whole new endeavor for me."

"Chuck, I am sure you will think of something."

"Maybe they will appreciate my Rock 'n Roll moves and impressions.

Chris laughing, "How about a Wild West Show?"

#

Chuck was observing.

"It looks like the park is filled with vendors, Chris," said Chuck, "with everything from Indian headdresses to the Fat Lady singing. Funeral home tents? Hahaha, they are everywhere, dotting the landscape, along with a bandstand. There is a snake oil salesman, look and there is a juggler, a yodeler, a car show, watermelon seed spitting contest, a womanless wedding, and three-leg races—even a tobacco spitting contest."

Smelling the popped corn through the trees, Chuck was patting himself on the back as he walked around the park. "Times like this always call for 'carney' food. Yep, red-skinned hot dogs, washtubs filled with ice-cold bottles of soft drink, and puke-pink cotton candy."

#

"Excuse me, sir, are you Reverend Gideon?"

"How can I help you?"

"I understand, Reverend, you have adopted a baby?"

"I don't believe I have met your acquaintance," said Gid.

"Oh, I apologize, my name is Chuck Converse. I do the local nightly news on Lighthouse Encounter Broadcasting. This story carries a lot of public interest. This is not something you see every day. I would appreciate an interview."

"Just what have you heard, Mr. Converse?"

"My sources tell me that you and your wife of fifty-five years are attempting to adopt a newborn baby."

"So, you believe that is interesting? People adopt babies every day."

"Yes, sir, I do, and the public is inquiring as to the truth of it all."

"And what, Mr. Converse, do you believe is interesting about this concept?"

"Reverend Gideon, we are going to turn the camera on, if you don't mind."

Chris proceeded to find a good camera angle showing the whitewashed oaks in the background, not knowing they would be a part of the conversation.

Beginning the interview with Gid and Purah, there was some cursory chitchat about the celebration before Chuck quickly focused on the adoption.

Gid knew this was, more than anything, an opportunity to talk about how God uses the weak things of this world to confound the wise.

"Reverend Gideon, our viewers are in amazement at the recent news about you and your wife adopting a newborn baby."

"Chuck, there is a lot of detail to this story, but to begin, the first thing I want to say, God does not fit into our boxes."

Chuck wasn't accustomed to talking about spiritual things, so his nervousness shone through. "Explain if you will what you mean by boxes."

"We tend to place constraints on Him based on what our own abilities have demonstrated."

"Oh, I see. You say, we try to make God be like us?"

"Realistically, I would not be one to advise this Parenting Paradox for others, nor did we pray to adopt a child. This is an example of God answering specific prayers of this group of people, who are viewed as useless to society. Useless, not because of some behavior, but for no other reason except age."

"Age must have some bearing, Reverend Gideon."

"There are many dynamics at play here, Chuck. Age is certainly one of them. Chuck, do you remember times with your grandparents?"

"Oh yes, they took time with me to teach me a lot of what I use today. Things that are practical."

"My point exactly, Chuck. There is some advantage to age. You learn by experience, to weed out things that don't matter. You learn to value and elaborate on the things that have enduring value.

"Our crew, we call them the Oaks, may not have *years*, but we have *time*. Does that make sense? No one knows the future. We don't know how long we will live, but we value our time and abilities. God hears our pleading prayers. He is giving us a battle, a *Closing Life-Challenge*."

"You say that as though it is a privilege to be adopting a newborn. I want to inject here: some have inferred that would be a burden."

"Reverend Gideon, this is much more than I could have imagined. It is intriguing. May we continue this interview on tomorrow's broadcast?"

"Certainly." Gid picked Charity Grace up in view of the camera.

With camera still on Charity Grace, "Our broadcast will continue tomorrow at the six o'clock hour. We will learn more about this *Closing Life-Challenge* of the 'Parenting Paradox.'"

#

"Reverend Gideon, I would like to continue right here, to simply record for tomorrow's broadcast. We can garner more viewers for this segment."

The interview continued, giving most of the known detail. "Reverend and Mrs. Gideon are pursuing the adoption of an infant girl. It seems they have a plan that was laid out by their 'Lord.'"

Gid added one comment that was a hook for the audience. "We are in a battle, our goal is in sight, but we have not yet made our first and ten, so to speak. Hehehe. We must find Charity Grace's father."

"So, Mrs. Gideon, what do you believe prepares you for this new chapter in your life?"

"We plan to keep doing what we have always done. Our lives are filled with thirsty students who, in a college setting, were preparing themselves for life. Daily, our home is filled with students we have mentored. Experience shows us how love nurtures the soul."

"Our *Closing Life-Challenge* will be our final battle. We realize this will involve potential for great difficulty. We have custody of our little girl now, yet nothing is final."

As the camera panned around to Chuck, he gave his closing comment. "Our coverage of the Parenting Paradox or what the Oaks call the *Closing Life-Challenge* will continue. Tomorrow, we will hear about Reverend Gideon's Harbor Oaks River Park encounter."

Chuck to his cameraman, "I knew this story had great potential as a human-interest story, but it could be the biggest thing I have ever done. We can follow the child with updates on milestones for years. We were first to break the story."

TV station switchboards could not handle the incoming calls. Many reports of possible fathers were coming in, with others offering to adopt the infant. Naysayers were strong too, pointing out the absurdity.

Countless advertisers were bidding for sponsorship. A fund was established for her college. Civic groups began to carry out projects at the assisted living community.

The story quickly gained national attention to the chagrin of DFS. They determined that this adoption must be settled promptly; however, the court was in control.

CHAPTER TWENTY-TWO
Papa Goes to Court

Blonde and fair-skinned, Dudley Taylor had lost his two bottom front teeth and wasn't at all embarrassed about it. Not a bad man, not a good man, but a catalyst drifting—without a compass or cause.

Soon, social workers were interviewing Dudley, (Papa) Taylor. "Yes, I have nine kids."

"Mr. Taylor, your last child is in a foster home?"

"No, ma'am. All nine of my kids are back home with me. After I was released from jail and rehab, I have been granted temporary custody."

"Mr. Taylor, our department believes that you have a newborn infant, born just before you were incarcerated, the day before your wife passed."

"Ma'am, I really don't know what yer talking 'bout. She never said nothing about another kid."

"Mr. Taylor, we believe her plans were to place that baby for adoption, without your knowledge."

"Well," after a long pause, "I just don't know what to do. I can't take care of a newborn baby and the rest of my brood."

"Sir, we have talked to the people who were caring for the child when your wife died. They have sworn under oath that this child was placed in their care by Rose Taylor, who worked at Harbor Oaks Assisted Living. Was Rose Taylor your wife?"

"Yes, Rosie was my wife. She was a good mama and a hard worker." Still grieving, he wiped tears on a snotty shirt. "I don't know what happened toer."

"Mr. Taylor, we have here a copy of Rose Taylor's death certificate."

"Let me see that. Does it tell what happened toer?"

"It says right here, Cause of death: hemorrhaging, secondary cause of death: obesity.'

"The baby was not born in a hospital. She left the baby with these people when she was approximately one day old. They later found a note she left stating her desire for them to raise her."

"Mr. Taylor, now that we have found you, we will have the judge schedule a hearing with you. You are the father. You have rights."

"This is just too much for me to understand, ma'am. So, what do you mean I have 'rights?'"

"Mr. Taylor, this is your baby. You are the legal 'responsible person,' no different than your other children."

"You can comply with your wife's wishes or not."

"Thank you, ma'am."

"Mr. Taylor, I will make my report back to the department and contact the judge. You will have a court-appointed attorney, to represent you. I will be in touch."

"I guess I would like to see my baby."

"Mr. Taylor, that will be easy to set up."

#

Dudley Taylor had thrown away his life with both hands. Walking slumped, up the path to Gid and Purah's apartment, he was a man whose life was riddled with bad decisions. Sober, he was, yet he felt the need for a drink. Sobriety was hard enough at best without such a weighty decision on his heart. He was trying to sort it all out, but the foreboding thought seemed to overrule. "I already have nine children at home, and I love them all."

"Good afternoon, Reverend and Mrs. Gideon, I would like for you to meet Dudley Taylor, Charity Grace's father."

Reaching for Purah's hand, "I am proud to meeche, ma'am."

Thinking to himself, *I didn't know Mr. Gideon was a preacher.*

Ms. Vermillia began the conversation, catching everyone up as far as who knew what. "As you know. Mr. Taylor wanted to see his daughter."

"Yes, this all really caught me by surprise."

Gid took his seat in a straight chair across from Mr. Taylor, leaning forward and looking him in the eye. "Sir, it has been our honor to be the caretakers of your precious daughter, who is now seven months old."

Purah, bringing in Charity Grace, "She is a beautiful, healthy child. She is settled into a routine with us including visitors who are teaching her to sing and giving her workouts. Her doctor says she is advanced for her age." Purah hands her to him, as Charity Grace made eye contact with him, cooing, and reaching for his nose.

"It seems like you folks were at the right place at the right time, for Rosie."

Dudley reaching for her. You could tell he was comfortable holding babies. "Baby girl, you're a shocker for this old boy. You be calling me Papa. I guess your mama sacrificed all she had for you."

"Yes, Mr. Taylor," Gid said. "We realize this is all in God's timing. We would have never planned any of this; however, our hearts have always been to offer ourselves to Him, our talents to Him—to do his will. Scripture gives us a basic plan for our lives, but God is the Captain of our ship. So, He is steering us into some deep water. We believe this is all part of His plan for Charity Grace."

"Charity Grace?"

"Yes, when Rose left her with us, she said to call her Charity Grace."

"She named all our babies. They all had special meaning. Do you know what she meant using that name?"

"She didn't say. However, on the evening she asked us to pray for her and her decision about the unborn baby, she was in our church service and heard the old ship's bell tolling—that now hangs in our church belfry. That bell came from the *Charity Grace*."

Hesitating, with a lump in his throat, as thoughts began to spin in his head, "I guess she didn't tell you that I had worked on that ship as a boy. The *Charity Grace* went down in a storm. It was a miracle that any of us survived."

"Mr. Taylor, she was honoring you with that name. She loved this baby girl. She just believed that the two of you could not raise another child."

"My thinking too, Reverend Gideon. I really dunno what I will do with our other nine. Two of 'em haven't started school.

"You don't know this, but I been in jail. The kids were in foster care. I wenta rehab and came home to this. I know I hafta stay sober now. I don't have Rosie ta lean on."

"Mr. Taylor, Listen to the note that Rose left in our linen. We didn't find it for a few days. By that time, we had learned of her passing. She wrote, 'I am so afraid for my baby. We just cannot raise another child. My husband does not work often. We have seven children in school and two at home. I want you good folks to do what is best for my baby girl. She needs your insight. I just want more for her.'"

"Charity Grace, you look just like our other children. I hate to even say this, but you must be mine. Course, none of them look like me—they all look like Rosie."

"Mr. Taylor, I want to share with you the things that have gone on here with us folks and the *Closing Life-Challenge*, that we believe God placed before us."

Vermillia rose to her feet and began to walk toward the door. "Reverend and Mrs. Gideon, Mr. Taylor needs time to assimilate all that transpired and for this part of your conversation. This could be construed as tort and he will need his attorney to advise him."

"Mr. Taylor, we want you to come back Monday afternoon and bring your other children. We will share with you at that time all that transpired, attorney or not," said Gid.

#

The Gideon living room was crowded with the Taylor children sitting in the floor and their attorney Mr. Slickman, Ms. Vermillia, as well as all the Oaks.

Purah suggested, "Let's all go down to the Harbor Oaks River Park."

Gid recounted the Hospice diagnosis, the meeting with the Lord, the teaching that Rose also heard, and all that had happened since the temporary guardianship of Charity Grace.

"Mr. Taylor, you do not need to make your decision yet. The Gideons will take care of Charity Grace until the hearing," added Attorney Slickman.

"Ms. Vermillia, if he wants to see her again, will you make the arrangements?"

"I will certainly make it a priority."

"Mr. Taylor, the court hearing is Thursday of next week. I will let you know what time," said Vermillia.

Vermillia, taking Charity Grace's hand, "She seems much better adjusted since she came back to you folks."

"We will talk soon, Reverend," said Vermillia.

#

"Ms. Vermillia, I think I'm gonna try to take her. My two big girls can help. I can get SSI on her too."

"Mr. Taylor, you do not need to decide today. After you have had time to sleep on this, come to my office tomorrow and we will go over the details."

"Ms. Vermillia, I will be in touch."

"You have my number, Mr. Taylor."

#

Vermillia walked in the door as her phone rang. "Ms. Vermillia, this is Mr. Slickman, the court-appointed attorney for Dudley Taylor. I have worked with the department on many cases, but this one takes the cake. I just want you to know, my advice to my client, Mr. Taylor, will be for placement. The judge can take it from there."

"Knowing that gives me peace, but I wonder about the other nine children," she said. "I know we will be following up on them for some time."

"Parents have rights, but children also have rights. Monitoring, counseling, and oversight will benefit them all, ma'am."

"Yes, but that is just the skeleton. Mr. Slickman, I understand what you are saying, but somebody will be responsible to put meat on the skeleton. Social services can only do so much. Her family will be shaping her personality, her creativity, her social interaction, and much more. There is much to be said for a loving stable home environment."

CHAPTER TWENTY-THREE
Charity Grace Goes to the Taylors

The girls were less than happy to have another sibling of which to take care. Getting up before daylight was interfering with their schoolwork. They had no skills to care for a baby. DFS was in the home frequently.

"Why is baby girl crying? Is she hungry?" said Papa.

"No, Daddy, she won't eat."

"We have to take her to the doctor appointment tomorrow," said Dud.

"Daddy, I think she is sick."

#

Fortunate for Dudley, with no driver's license, Dr. Edmonds' office was in walking distance. Dr. Edmonds' kind blue eyes and bushy eyebrows captivated his patients.

"Mr. Taylor, I am Dr. Edmonds. I am Charity Grace's pediatrician."

"Doc, I think she is sick. She won't eat, and she cries all the time."

Concerned, "You are right. She is dehydrated. Let me check her out. Maybe we can find the problem."

"Nurse, please call the hospital. We will need to send her over for fluids and bloodwork."

"Mr. Taylor, I am going to recommend that she go back to the Gideons for now."

"Doc, have we done something wrong?"

"Nurse, get DFS on the phone, please.

"Hello, Ms. Vermillia, this is Dr. Edmonds. The Taylor baby must go back to the Gideons. Once again, she is failing to thrive. We are admitting her to the hospital, get the Gideons over at once."

"Mr. Taylor," said Dr. Edmonds, "her anxiety is keeping her from taking nourishment. This is critical. She will die if we let this situation continue. I am terribly sorry."

#

In the courtroom were the Oaks, as they had always been for the hearings.

The juvenile judge was long tenured and knew Reverend Gideon from past testimonies given about abuse and neglect observations in his ball players.

"All rise. The honorable Judge Pharness Thomas presiding," said the court's clerk.

Pounding the gavel, "This court will now come to order."

"Mr. Taylor, please approach the bench."

"Yes, Your Honor."

"Please state your full name."

"Uh, my name is Dudley Taylor."

"Mr. Taylor, what is your relationship to Charity Grace Taylor?"

"Judge, she's my daughter."

"Mr. Taylor, I have been involved in this case for some time now. The fact that you are her father gives you legal rights. You were permitted to take her home on a provisional basis, to be with the rest of your children.

"Charity Grace Taylor is an infant. She does not have the ability to care for herself. She is a dependent child.

"Charity Grace Taylor is bonded with the Gideons. Placement in two other homes each caused her condition to become critical.

"Mr. Taylor, you are not capable of caring for her at this time. Your other children cannot be relied on to provide her care, as they are young and inexperienced."

"Mr. Taylor, you are the responsible party, not your other children. It is your responsibility to nurture and provide for your children. Agreed, you do not have a wife in the home. However, the state provides income for your family, enabling you to be in the home full-time. Having an infant to care for, along with your other responsibilities, is not meeting even her basic needs.

"Reverend and Mrs. Gideon, will you approach the bench."

"Yes, sir, Your Honor."

"Reverend and Mrs. Gideon, I am giving the two of you guardianship of Charity Grace Taylor, until such time Mr. Taylor decides to voluntarily either place her with you or place her with the State.

"Mr. Taylor, if you fail for any reason to voluntarily place her, the State will terminate your rights. The court will revisit this matter in one month."

"Judge Thomas, we thank you," said Reverend Gideon.

"Court is adjourned."

The Oaks let out a cheer and surrounded the Gideons in celebration.

Miller, running with his arms held high, "My prayer for her—she is not traumatized."

Ochre whispered to David, "She might benefit from counseling as time goes by. Nobody knows how these things affect children."

"Now Ochre, how is she going to tell a counselor how traumatized she is? Maybe she can talk to you, the way Scruffy does."

"David, they have their ways. Counselors know what to look for."

CHAPTER TWENTY-FOUR
Outings for the Siblings.

Dudley Taylor's attorney had scheduled a meeting with Reverend and Mrs. Gideon.

"Reverend and Mrs. Gideon, I have been in discussion with Mr. Dudley Taylor about Charity Grace's placement, said Mr. Slickman. My recommendation to him is to permanently place her with you, by permanent guardianship.

"The judge may not approve of this, but Mr. Taylor does not want to lose contact with her."

"So, you mean he is not terminating his rights?"

"Exactly. He can later petition the court for custody. It doesn't mean custody would ever be granted to him. However, that would still be on the table. The judge may never even acknowledge his petition. That is his decision. The court date is set for day after tomorrow."

#

"This court is now in session. The Honorable Judge, Pharness Thomas now presides, said the Clerk of Court."

"Reverend and Mrs. Gideon, will now approach the bench, said Judge Thomas."

167

"You understand, Reverend and Purah Gideon, Dudley Taylor wants to give you permanent guardianship of Charity Grace Taylor, with visitation rights?"

"Yes, sir, we do."

Privately, "I am going to rule that the State sever his paternal rights, to allow you to adopt her. You will be allowed to determine whether he can have visitation rights. This child does not need to be a pawn of his, for her entire childhood."

"Mr. Dudley Taylor, will you approach the bench, please?"

"Mr. Taylor, the State of Georgia is permanently severing your rights and responsibilities of Charity Grace Taylor. You will have no further contact with her unless granted by her adoptive parents.

"Reverend and Mrs. Gideon, the State hereby awards permanent parenthood to you of Charity Grace.

"Your attorneys will take care of paperwork. Do any of you have questions? Certainly, Reverend Gideon?"

"To Mr. Taylor, I would like to say that we will arrange for you and your other children to visit her."

Judge Thomas rose. "Charity Grace Taylor is now legally Charity Grace Gideon. Court adjourned."

#

Gid speaking, "Mr. Taylor, it is our desire for Charity Grace to know you and her brothers and sisters. We will develop times of interaction for you all. She will always know her life story."

"Reverend Gideon, I dunno what to say. This is the best I cudda hoped for. This'll mean so much to my other kids. They've grieved for their mother. They don't understand all that is hap'nin'. Thankye, agin."

"We are thankful that you approve. Please know we want the best for your entire family too. We will be in touch soon."

As Dudley turned to walk away, he took a deep, slow breath, "God, I don't usuly pray, but this is a good hap'nin'. I'm sorry for making my girls tryta take keer uh her. I hope they don't fee lak it's ther fault. I am sorry fur wantin' that xtre check, too."

CHAPTER TWENTY-FIVE
Ochre's Pendulum Is Swinging Back

Finding the archives for the 'Friday' paper was a long sought-after piece of Ochre's past.

Okay. Here we are. This paper sure changed. These pages are so much bigger—hm, brown and brittle and funky smelling.

Ochre slowly turned pages, noticing the old photos.

"Here it is, here it is!"

#

OBITUARIES

May 7, 1924
Arrangements for Gordon 'Snitch' Pollard who collapsed at the Church social on Saturday night are incomplete.
Infant Timbrok
Graveside service was held on Thursday morning at Eastern Sky Cemetery for the stillborn infant son of Chet and Eliza Timbrok.
He is survived by 4 brothers and 4 sisters. The ladies Sunday School Class of Zion Church were the flower bearers.
Annabelle Eula Watkins
The arrangements for Mrs. Newton Watkins whose soul left this world on Friday last, are incomplete, waiting the body's return from the crime lab.

"Snitch" Pollard, incomplete, Infant Timbrok, and Annabelle Eula Watkins.

I guess I forgot her name was Annabelle. Daddy always called her Sweet Annie.

Snitch died of possible poisoning. That is interesting. Annabelle Eula Watkins died of undetermined causes. I wonder if there is an associated article with their death.

Here is the gossip column.

#

NEIGHBORHOOD GOSSIP INSIDER

The news was delivered today by Harbor Oaks telephone operator Weezy Walker, of the birth of the Watkins baby, along with the sad news of the mother's death, Sweet Annie.

Sweet Annie was found soon after her death by loving husband Newt.

Poor Newt was so overcome with grief when he was later found by his cousin Gladys. Newt was grasping his newborn baby so tightly, while slumped over Annie's body, that Gladys had to pry that baby out of Newt's arms.

Gladys left them alone with Annie's "crazy" mother, to carry the news to the city and Justice of the Peace, Dover. He went out with Sheriff Fraker and Coroner Hall to muster up a jury and hold an inquest. Gladys told everybody, "I spect her crazy Mama gave her poison."

Dear Annie will be sweetly missed. She will be long remembered for her winning knack for snuff spittin' and picklin' pigs' feet.

In other news, Snitch Pollard flopped over Saturday, after the social. He was carried home in Old Bill's wagon, where he later died. Doc Blackford was sent after but was unable to save Snitch.

Doc was overheard saying, "His death looks mighty like a poison death. I am suspicious of what he ate at the social."

Snitch knew everybody and was a buddy to the locals, men, and women, down at The Tavern. He was famous for carrying gossip to the communities.

\#

Now what is this? This looks like a good piece to the puzzle.

CORONER INQUEST

Coroner Hall ruled the death of Annabelle Eula Watkins as death by poison, based on the crime lab autopsy.

The circumstances of the death are believed to be malicious according to Sheriff Fraker. Mrs. Watkins' caregiver, Gladys Watkins, has been charged with Involuntary Manslaughter.

Immediately, a witness to the mode of death was found.

Gladys Watkins has been bound over to the Grand Jury. The circumstances around *believed* death of Gordon Pollard were noted as essential and contributed to the charges of Gladys Watkins.

\#

And what would our town do without our gossips? thought Ochre.

NEIGHBORHOOD GOSSIP INSIDER

Weezy Walker reported that Snitch Pollard was not dead after all. Snitch learned at The Tavern: Gladys Watkins came in bragging that she was going to marry her cousin. She said, "The Watkins folks always marry our cousins."

When Snitch put 2 and 2 together, he came up with what her plan was.

When he heard Sweet Annie died, he knew he needed to do something.

Everybody knows loose lips sink ships. I guess she was getting up her courage. She kept talking about fish milk poison.

At the Church Social, she wouldn't leave Snitch alone until he ate her fish milk soup.

\#

Hm, looks like old Snitch knew he was the only one who would have figured out her plan, thought Ochre. He took a bowl and faked eating it.

Snitch must have been pret-ty shrewd. I bet he was a frequent snitch. So, he went right then and talked to Sheriff Fraker. They decided to fake his poisoning, to take her off guard. It worked. Who would ever know she poisoned Snitch? Then, blaming Mama's "crazy mama" almost worked.

They had the evidence, though. The crime lab analyzed Snitch's soup and found fish milk poison. It would have all remained a mystery if Snitch had not been at the tavern that night.

Don't God work in mysterious ways.

\#

Finally, now I think I can piece enough of this together to understand the circumstances of Mama's death.

\#

SEED-SPITTIN' CONTEST

REGISTRATION is now underway for the annual watermelon seed-spittin' contest at the local WATERMELON FEST, on Friday night of next week.

Many regional spitters will be on hand to demonstrate their skills, with the state contest winner from last year leadin' off the event, Mr. Mill Waits.

Ole Mill stated, "Hardworking people should enter the event 'cause they have large lungs." Mr. Waits has challenged the Chorister at Zion Church to a "spit contest." Winner will receive a jackknife.

Contestants will be required to bring their own watermelon. The local FFA will be sponsoring this event with prizes up to $25 for division winners.

Registration fee is one dollar per event. Categories include male 12-17, female12-17, also male and female children ages 8 to 11.

Tobacco spitters will compete in the adult categories only. That event will be held on Saturday night. Spittin' seminars will be held on Saturday morning to teach the art of tobacco spittin'. This seminar will be led by "Chip the Lip" Pollard. Chip the Lip says, "Develop yer technique while yer young."

Proceeds from these events will benefit the local FFA club. Prize money furnished by Creek Bottoms Feed and Seed.

I'm getting off track. I can come back later.

Cousin Gladys thought she could marry Daddy. She must have been obsessed with that and saw this as her opportunity. I always wondered about her disappearance. It had to come at her arrest. She would have never left, after Mama died.

But "fish milk soup"? That took some creativity. I will investigate that one. Then, what was her sentence? There should be more in Weezy's gossip column, for sure.

This is enough for me to assimilate right now. I will come back later for more gossip.

#

Driving to the old cabin, "Mama, I am coming to see you."

Opening the car door, Ochre slowly swung his left leg out of the car. "Maybe I can manage to stand up here."

Holding onto the car, looking down into the Holler, and taking a deep breath, he thought, *this will be a cleansing for me. I am going to take my time today and look at everything at Granny's cabin with new eyes.*

"Daddy and Mama, I guess I will be exhuming your remains, or maybe not." Walking on around the graves of his sisters, "I will call that developer and let him know I am ready to sell."

Holding onto the rotted porch post, "With any luck, this floor will hold me one last time.

"I think I will keep this old table where Mama died, or maybe not. I need something uplifting.

"What I see now is my painful past, Lord. I am leaving this today and allowing you to heal me completely."

Ochre heard an engine shut off.

I wonder who that is? No one knows I am here.

Gid was musing, *coming over here may not be an encouragement for Ochre at all. LORD, help him find a way to let go of this place.*

This time, I will park beside these tomb rocks and go up from the side of the porch. Purah was right. Creepy does not describe this plaaace. "Ohh, Ohh!"

Ochre made his way to the door.

"Gid, Gid, is that you? What happened? Where are you?

"Gid, I hear you. Where are you? Oh, no, not the well!"

"Ochre, you can't help me out."

Then, through the timbers, Ochre could see light shining on his face.

"Oh, Gid, I am so sorry. That well should have been marked with something.

"I will have to leave you down there, to go get help. Gid, the fire department is just over the hill. They can help."

"Ochre, I am in nasty water up to my waste."

Ochre was moving like a turtle.

This is taking him an eternity, thought Gid.

If this had happened sixty years ago, it would be funny, thought Ochre. *I hope he is not hurt.*

Last time he was here, I was laughing about the Hague. Now, I am laughing about him falling into the well because of my stupidity.

Gid was thinking. *I am probably in a snake den along with parasites and who knows what else.*

"What is this? Ochre Watkins, it is bones. So, I am not the only one in here. Ohh. Dear God, please put your hedge of protection around me."

Gid stuck his arm through the broken timbers and attempted to toss the bone out.

#

The fire department arrived and began removing the rotted timbers from the well opening.

"Reverend Gideon, can you slip this rope under your arms?"

"Yes, I believe I can."

"Boys, you just won't believe what I found in there," said Gid.

"Are you injured?

"Just my pride.

"Just when I thought it was the nastiest place ever, I felt what looked like an arm bone."

"Um, I see that. Reverend Gideon, we will call the sheriff."

"Sheriff, for what?" said Gid.

"Those bones look like human bones," said the EMT.

Gid said, "Oh, I can hear Purah now. 'Nobody but you, Gid.'

"Take me to the ER. I need to be decontaminated."

"Sir, we will need to decontaminate you here on the spot. We will shower you with high-volume, low-pressure, then take you to the hospital."

#

All the while, Ochre was sitting in his car and oblivious to the findings.

I will return here to sign the sale agreement and allow LaMarah to see it one last time. The thing for me to do now would be follow the ambulance to the hospital. I can call Purah from there.

#

Hurrying to answer the phone, "Yes, Sheriff, this is Mrs. Purah Gideon. Where is he? Is he okay?"

Then calling Maude, "Oh, Maude, can you babysit? Gid had an accident. They think he will be okay."

#

Gid filled Purah in on the events of the day.

"Leave it to you, Gid," said Purah. "You are always in the right place at the right time. So, whose bones might they be?"

"The sheriff needed to talk to Ochre first and get his take on that," said Gid.

About that time in walked Ochre.

"Ochre, this has been a day of it."

"Gid, you don't know the half of it. I decided to sell the homeplace and all this happened."

"Ochre, the bones may not want you to sell," laughed Gid.

"Gid, this is odd," said Ochre. The sheriff is going to see if there are any reports of missing people. We may never know who it was. Hm, missing people?"

#

"LaMarah, this is Dad. I need you to plan on coming soon. I have some business that I want you to help me take care."

"Dad, are you okay?"

"Yes, I am truly experiencing release from the bitterness that kept me bound all these years. I just have some processes to go through."

"Yes, I can come next weekend if that will work for you. I will be there Friday morning."

"Dad, have you seen a doctor yet?"

"Not yet. I will make a doctor appointment today."

"That is what I needed to hear, Dad. See you then."

#

"Pansie, I have made an appointment with my primary care physician to find out what is causing my stiffness and speech problems."

"Ochre, we do need to know. It could be something treatable, or even curable."

"It's possible. That is what I am hoping for," Ochre said.

"I just talked to LaMarah. She put me on the spot about making an appointment. I asked her to come soon."

"I have finally decided to sell the homeplace. She doesn't know that, but I told her I needed her to help with some business. It will be a good time to take care of my living will, and Durable Power of Attorney for healthcare, too."

"Ochre, you are making real progress."

"Yes, I just can't tell you how much better I feel, emotionally. I was really in a pit. I had nothing to live for."

"Now, we have LaMarah back," said Pansie. "Our lives seem to have purpose again."

CHAPTER TWENTY-SIX
Eviction

"Unca Miller, brush your teeth!"

"Are they dirty, baby girl?"

Putting her hand over her mouth, "I think it's funny," she said.

Teasingly, "And why is that?

"'Cause you take them out of your mouth."

Miller, struggling to keep a straight face, remembered when she may have seen him brushing his teeth. "I don't let anybody see me brush my teeth but you, Baby. I love you so much, I would do anything for you."

"I remember you put me on the counter when you would brush your teeth," she said.

"You can't remember that far back. You were just a baby," he said. "Okay, here goes."

Maude walked in to see what the party was all about. "I have never heard so much foolishness, Miller. What are you doing to her? Laughing has given her hiccups!"

"Okay, you brush your teeth and see what she does."

"You two are full of foolishness. She had poor ole David going this morning," said Maude.

She said, "Patting David's bald head, 'Where is you haya?'"

"David said, 'It is in the floor at the barbershop.'"

"'Let's go get it.'"

"So, what did they do," asked Miller?

"The story I got, "'Mr. Converse was putting his cigarette out, just as we were walking in. He blew out a huge puff of smoke," said David.

"Charity Grace climbed up in his lap, sucking her index finger with her other fingers resting on her nose. She got right in his face, pooched out her lips, and said, 'Smoking is doorty'."

"I don't know if we should be embarrassed or laugh, Miller."

"Maude, what did he say?"

"He said, 'Charity Grace, if you say it is doorty, then it *is* doorty. I guess I will have to quit that.'

"Everybody is so understanding. Her frontal lobes are still developing. Her judgment is not the best."

"Maude, she gives all of us so much joy. We have all fallen in love with that little darling."

#

Chuck wanted to set up the next interview in Zion Chapel, with a clip of David leading the choir, then Reverend Gideon preaching. He managed to get a shot of Miller swinging his crooked arm as he was shouting and praising the Lord.

The camera showed the Gideons walking out of the Sanctuary with Charity Grace.

Chuck orienting the TV viewers, "Reverend and Mrs. Gideon recently finalized the adoption of the newborn infant who was left with them.

"Mrs. Gideon, How old is Charity Grace now?"

"I can't believe it, Chuck. She is already two years old."

"Mrs. Gideon, tell us how you feel, now that the adoption is final."

"Chuck, people are showing such concern for us and Charity Grace. A few are appalled that people our age are allowed to adopt a newborn baby."

"Mrs. Gideon, how have you responded to the negativity?"

"Chuck, there isn't any need to respond. If they truly are concerned, God will show them His wisdom in this exceptional story.

"As you know, our prayers are to be able to leave what we are with someone so that the things God endows us with will pass along to others, very much in the way you would see a runner pass a baton. What we are doing is investing in the life of Charity Grace. Her life will draw the dividends and interest of our principal investment. And Chuck, it will not just end there. She too will invest in the lives of others."

Purah, looking into the camera, "Each person listening to this interview is investing in the lives of others. It is like planting seeds. The seeds you plant are the seeds that sprout and grow. The fruit they bear will either benefit others or be an affliction to them. Please ask yourself, for what will you be remembered?"

"Reverend Gideon, this is so thought-provoking. In what way will this all come about?"

"You see, Chuck, Charity Grace came to us a blank canvas. We are taking the brushes of our lives and creating a glorious masterpiece. I suppose there are many ways to describe what God is allowing here. We are skillfully applying different hues and textures to her life. Only

God knows of the finished work, for it is his hand that is guiding ours."

"Reverend Gideon, this just keeps getting better."

The camera panned around to Chuck. "I learned at the barbershop yesterday from this little darling that 'smoking is doorty.' Based on that, I have decided to give up smoking.

"The next segment, we want to talk about the Oaks' interaction with Charity Grace Gideon and what she is learning. Ladies and gentlemen, we will return here next week, where age is just a number and parenting is a journey. Where will that journey lead the Gideon family?"

#

"Gid, it has been a long day. We need to open the mail before we get ready for bed. I will bathe Charity Grace and you can do the honors with the mail."

Enjoying the honors. "This one is from Harbor Oak Assisted Living.

Dear Mr. and Mrs. Gideon,

It has been our honor here at Harbor Oaks Assisted Living Community to have the two of you as residents. Your presence and interaction are a true asset to the family here.

We regret to inform you, based on your admission agreement, we will not be renewing your lease. The agreement strictly states residents must be over 18 years of age who live here.

Given the fact you have adopted a child, you no longer meet the lease requirements.

We will assist you in finding other housing if need be. Please let us know if you need our assistance, in this matter.

Vigil Hatch

"Dear Lord, what are you about to accomplish with this move? Should we appeal, or comply? I know your hand is in this."

Turning his head to the bedroom door, Gid began to verbalize his anxiety. "Purah, baby, I have some disturbing news. I really don't know what to make of it."

"What can be so bad, Gid? We have fought a lot of battles. God is not forsaking us."

"I know, Baby. This letter just came from the home here."

"Let me see it."

After reading, "Gid, this could turn out for our good. We just need to trust God."

"Remind me, Purah, to open mail in the mornings. I won't sleep a wink tonight."

"You remember, Gid, Mrs. Morrison cautioned us at our first meeting about Charity Grace, that this was a possibility?"

"You are right. God is never caught by surprise. His plan will unfold in the next few days."

CHAPTER TWENTY-SEVEN
Lighthouse Gossip

"Are the Oaks all here?"

David was leaned into Ochre and Scruffy to see if he could hear what Scruffy was saying, while Dr. and Mrs. Morrison were playing with Charity Grace on the sofa.

Ochre said, "Excuse you, Scruffy."

"What did he do?" asked David.

"Didn't you hear that burp?"

"Dogs don't burp."

"Ochre, said Maude, "it is about time you got checked out by your doctor. You just can't keep going like this."

"You are right. LaMarah called my hand on it, and I promised to make an appointment, which I did. Hope to know something soon."

"LaMarah is coming home next weekend. We will have to plan some time with all the Oaks."

"Scruffy," said Ochre, "why am I the only one you lick on the face?"

David said, "He likes to lick the food off your beard, ah ha."

#

"As you all know, I am investigating the circumstances surrounding my mother's death. The *Lighthouse News and Views* newspaper contains some interesting articles. The most interesting stories are in the gossip column. You get more news there than from official sources."

"Ochre," said Maude, "are you learning what you need to know?"

"I am beginning to get some detail. Why haven't you ever asked me about it?"

"Ochre, I heard gossip over the years. I don't know how much of it is true."

"Did you all hear gossip? You never told me. Shouldn't you tell me?"

Gid said, "Ochre, gossip is not worthy of discussing. If it were wrong, it would distress you for no reason. It is better that you find it out from true sources, the way you are doing now."

"Yes, I know you are all right. Pansie, did you hear gossip?"

"No, Ochre, but I did always speculate why the creek was called Fish Milk Creek. What on earth is fish milk? Does that have anything to do with anything?"

"Apparently, my mama was poisoned with fish milk."

"Daddy's cousin Gladys was charged, but never arrested, with her poisoning."

"Finally. So, do you know what happened?" said Pansie.

"Oh, but there is more. Cousin Gladys was planning to marry Daddy, and she also tried to poison Snitch Pollard. She tried to blame my 'Cr-azy Granny' who had dementia, with Mama's death. Snitch figured it all out and went to the sheriff."

"Wow," said Mrs. Morrison, "that would make a great movie."

Things quieted as everyone turned their attention to Scruffy, as he was contending for attention. Again, David was leaning in to hear Scruffy's conversation with Ochre.

"Scruffy, show David how you can spit tobacco into your new spittoon."

Scruffy jammed his nose into the spittoon. "David," said Ochre, "sit down, you will distract him. He would be embarrassed if you knew he dips."

"Ochre heard Scruffy say, 'Ochre, that rat just crawled into your pocket.'"

"A rat!" Jerking off his shirt, "Did y'all see a rat?"

CHAPTER TWENTY-EIGHT
Ochre's Doctor Appointment

Ochre registered with the doctor's receptionist and shuffled to an armchair.

"Ochre, what did Scruffy say to you at Gid's?"

"Pansie, you know Scruffy doesn't talk."

"Oh, really?"

"David thinks he does."

"Ochre, you need to tell the doctor about your hallucinations and delusions. They are coming more severe."

Swinging open the door, "Mr. Ochre Watkins, come this way and we will get your weight."

After the medical history and neurological exam, the doctor ordered several lab tests as well as a brain imaging study. "Mr. Watkins, have you shown any signs of delusions or hallucinations?"

"None that I know of."

Cutting her eyes, Pansie said, "Doctor, Ochre thinks Scruffy talks to him."

"Who is Scruffy, Ochre?"

"Scruffy is my friend's dog."

"Does Scruffy talk to you?"

"Yes, he does."

"What kind of things does he say?"

"Do you think I am crazy, Doc?"

"Mr. Watkins, delusions and hallucinations are common with certain neurological diseases. They can be treated."

"Scruffy told me I had a rat in my pocket."

At this point, the doctor had to turn his head to keep Ochre from seeing him grin. He said, "Ochre, make an appointment next Friday morning for a report on your test results, and give my regards to Scruffy."

"Pansie, I am glad that is over. I am anxious for my diagnosis. So, what am I going to do without Scruffy talking to me?"

Jokingly, "That will give you more time to terrorize David."

"David likes to hear what Scruffy says."

"You two will have to find something else to pass your time," said Pansie.

"Yeah," said Ochre, "like putting snakes in flutes."

CHAPTER TWENTY-NINE
Hanai Adoption

The Taylor children were showing a lot of interest in learning new things. Their change of environment on Wednesdays was proving to benefit both them and the Oaks.

Ricky was learning his guitar chords and finger patterns very quickly. David was eager to teach him the traditional folk songs. "David, do you think you can teach me 'Achy Breaky Heart'?"[54]

"Ricky, are you having love problems?"

"It's just a fun song."

Becca was becoming quite a tennis player. She was running every day to build stamina. "Doc Morrison, what should I eat? I want to be strong and healthy."

An onlooker would feel sorry for Miller. He was limping and broken everywhere you could see.

Miller let go of the reins and said, "Easy, Ranger, be easy on Cal."
"Keep his head up, Cal."

---

[54] (Tress 1990)

Cal was learning about farming and horseback riding. "Miller, I want to be a roper and barrel racer. Is this the kind of horse for that?"

"Cal, you are just learning to stay on a horse right now. Let us take it one day at a time. We will get there, Little Fellar."

Ernest was a studious boy. "Mrs. Morrison, how do you know when a person is guilty? I don't see anything in these books that teaches that."

"An attorney's job is to represent their client, Ernest, guilty or not. If we could determine their guilt or innocence, we would only need judges, not a jury—or attorneys, for that matter. The only one who knows a person's innocence or guilt is our creator, God."

Charity Grace's siblings were bonding with her, as well as all the Oaks. Wednesdays were like a celebration for the Oaks. Pouring themselves into the children was a bit sporadic, with it all coming together one day a week.

If they were not instructing, they were there cheering the children on.

#

"Gid," said Purah, "Suzanne came by today. She was telling me about a tradition that the Hawaiians hold dear to their heart. 'Their understanding of adoption is different from ours.' She personally had adopted over a hundred Hanai children."

"Sometimes it is a family member, often it is not. They may raise the child or maybe just help with their needs. The bond is between both families. It is an informal adoption called Hanai."[55]

Purah commented, "Gid, we never even considered this factor in our *Closing Life-Challenge*. This is another phenomenon of the

---

[55] (Maurer n.d.)

Parenting Paradox. This adoption seems to be breaking all precedence. Most adoptions remove the child from all connections. Not only are the Taylor children benefiting from this newfound relationship, the perception and guidance of the saged Oaks is proving to be a valuable mentorship for her siblings and us."

"Purah, God is weaving our past into this part of the relationship."

"These are the things we have always done, with new life and direction being infused into who we are."

"This is just another battlefront for us warriors, Purah."

"Our standard is love. There are many ways to demonstrate the fundamentals. With what we have been given, we are guaranteed victory. Love conquers."

CHAPTER THIRTY
Ben's Adoption

"Purah, look who's coming down the path. Is that Dr. Solomon? He must be paying a social visit. He discharged me last year."

"Gid, that is him. I know his spirit brought him here today. He must have something important—to tell us."

"Charity Grace, here is your ball cap. You better tie that shoe before you fall," said Gid.

#

"Reverend Gideon, Mrs. Gideon, how are you both doing?"

Purah could not wait for Gid to respond, "Dr. Solomon, we are so pleased to see you." Reaching for his hand with both of hers, "We just couldn't be better. Just how is the world treating you?"

"Dr. Solomon, what brings you back to our little neck of the woods?"

"I could say it was Nathaniel's pie, but that is only half of it. Gid, I must admit, I am intrigued by your improvement, as well as fascinated with what you called your *Closing Life-Challenge*. I was making a visit nearby and thought I would call on you."

As Dr. Solomon began to ask them questions, about how the *Closing Life-Challenge* was associated with the adoption and Reverend Gideon's health, his interest seemed to turn to his own adoption.

Taking a deep breath while leaning back, then forward, "Reverend Gideon, you know I have been researching my own adoption. I have concluded, the woman whom you mentioned at our last meeting is my mother, LaMarah. What I want to know from you Reverend Gideon, is that a possibility?"

"Dr. Solomon, tell me what you know, if you will."

"My adoptive parents have both passed. I have little information about my biological mother and father."

"It was when I introduced myself to you as Benjamin LaMar Solomon," clearing his throat, "I apologize. I normally keep my composure better than this."

"Do you remember your response?"

"Why, yes I do. I simply said, Ben, son of LaMar, son of LaMarah."

"Yes, exactly."

"My parents must have done that to give me a hint. I have searched different registries. There really aren't many LaMarahs."

"So, Reverend Gideon, the last time I saw you, it seemed you made a point to tell me, not so much about that delicious pie, but that LaMarah had been here the day before."

"Reverend Gideon, do you know something that I should know?"

"Ben, I have some puzzle pieces, but I haven't put them all together. I have not been sure if it was circumstantial or God moving once again. Purah and I have been pondering what to do. You know as a pastor; I don't divulge things I am told in confidence."

"Reverend, I would like to meet this LaMarah."

"I noticed your ball cap, Ben. Did you intern at Xandy?"

"No, I believe LaMarah works there."

"It is time you meet the Oaks, Ben. Why don't you have dinner with us Friday evening? LaMarah will be there."

CHAPTER THIRTY-ONE
Ochre's Breakthrough

"Ochre, I am glad you made the appointment so that LaMarah could be there," said Pansie, while pouring Ochre's morning coffee, out on the veranda.

"Yes, I have decided, we need to be living like a family."

"LaMarah, come on in. You have time for a cup of coffee. Your Dad is sitting on the veranda enjoying his morning view of the river park."

"Dad, you say you had a thorough work-up last week with the neurologist?"

"Yes, dear, he is supposed to have some answers for us today."

"That should give you some relief. Don't you think, Dad?"

"I really dread what he might say."

"Look out, LaMarah, there is a rat," weakly shuffling to get away from it.

Ochre flipped his chair over with his emotions rampant. Yelling, "Don't let it come near me!"

Helping him up, "Daddy, are you, all right? Your murophobia is out of control. There is no rat."

"Think about this, Dad. It is one thing to have a fear of rats; it is another to have delusions about them."

"You two, we are going to be late. Let's go," said Pansie.

"Daddy, you have declined since I saw you last. Let me put your feet into the car."

#

"Mr. Watkins, we have all your reports back. There is one more definitive test I will order. I will have our nurse make the appointment for you. It is a lumbar puncture, or spinal tap."

"I believe you have a condition called Normal Pressure Hydrocephalus, or NPH as it is often called."

"I was so afraid I had Parkinson's disease, Doc. Is this worse or better?"

"If it is in fact NPH, treatment involves surgically placing a shunt in your skull to drain the fluid. You will be able to lead a normal life with few limitations. This, however, does not explain the delusions."

"Doc, I am not delusional. Scruffy does talk."

Laughing, "Mr. Watkins, I will contact you when I receive the results from your test."

#

"LaMarah, I kinda like having you put my feet in the car."

"Pansie, let's drive over to the homeplace," said Ochre.

LaMarah was feeling a bit overwhelmed. It was still early in the day and so much had already happened.

"LaMarah, I have decided to sell the homeplace. I have been effectively dealing with the loss of my mother, my childhood, and the bitterness I had toward my father. It is time I sell that place and move on.

"Pansie, take it slow, around this drive, and pull up as close as you can to Granny's house.

"I just want us to have one last look at everything."

"Daddy, have you thought about the family cemetery here?"

"Yes," looking at each marker, "I thought I would have them all exhumed and bury them in a family plot at the church. What do you think?"

"Daddy, that is disturbing to think about. I guess it would be best. I just don't want to be around when you do it."

"Poor Gid fell in the well out here a couple of weeks ago. You will never believe what he found down in there."

"Is he okay, Daddy?"

"Yes, but as always, he helped open up a can of worms. He found a human bone down in there."

"Ssssooo? What do you know about that?"

#

"Here comes Matt. He is the developer. For years he's been trying to buy this place," said Ochre.

"Come in, Matt. This is my wife Pansie and my daughter LaMarah."

"Matt, what do you plan on doing with this place?" asked Pansie.

"I have plans to build thirty garden apartments on the creekbank and a subdivision there in the grove of pines."

"Matt," said Ochre, "I am having those pines harvested. That is the last phase of my retirement plan. My teacher Mr. Everette Weeks gave me that idea, back in grade school."

"Great, that will give me a head start," said Matt. "They would need to be cut before construction could begin."

Shaking hands with Matt, "I will meet with you next week. Let me know when you schedule the closing."

"LaMarah, let's get back for lunch to see what Nathaniel has cooked up. Remind me to ask if any of them know how Fish Milk Creek received its name. The Oaks will all be there—maybe one of them will know."

#

"Nathaniel, you are looking sharp today, with that houndstooth check on your coat pockets and pants. Do you dress like that all the time?" said LaMarah.

"Ms. LaMarah, I did it for you, 'cause I don't get to see you offen. Guess I be celebratin'."

"Nathaniel, you've made me feel special and we haven't even eaten yet. So, what is on the menu?"

Ochre chimes in, "I'm hungry for some collard greens."

"Now Ochre, you know your doctor won't letchu have dat. It gets tangled up with yo medicine."

Gid put his fingers over his lips, covering a grin while raising his eyebrows. "Nathaniel, we appreciate how you take such good care of us."

"Dats what I'm here fo. I did make y'alles favorites, Unca Gid. I dun got sum macaroni and cheese and warm, ho-made banana puddin' with sho nuff real meringue."

"Nathaniel, you are one in a million. Not only do you cook all our favorites, but you also keep up with our ailments too," said David. "How do you do that?

"Mr. David, I try too. Sometimes y'all mek me crazy. It's servin' time."

Ochre leaned over and whispered to Nat, "I want to borrow that wig."

"Ochre, nuf said. You know where yo bread is buttered," said Nathaniel.

Gid motioning, "Miller, will you say grace?"

#

Ochre began, "I brought LaMarah here today because I need to take care of some personal business. I want you all to know I have decided to sell the homeplace."

"What brought this on?" asked Dr. Morrison.

Half standing, "Folks, as you all know, I have been investigating my mother's death. There were things I just didn't know, even though it all happened so many years ago."

"One thing that is still unclear, did 'Fish Milk Creek' get named for the poison or was that already the name?"

"I found myself holding on to Granny's house more than anything, because that is where Mama died.

"Gid's sermon on forgiveness was what I needed to hear to get me over the hump. Once I forgave my father for neglecting me during my childhood, the issues began to dissolve because the bitterness was gone."

"Daddy, don't you think you will miss going over there?"

Slowly sitting back down, "Baby, in my mind, I have beat that dark horse to death. I can pass by there and enjoy the new development that is going in, now.

"LaMarah and Pansie went with me to the neurologist today, and he believes that I have a condition called Normal Pressure Hydrocephalus, or NPH. It is caused from fluid and pressure in the skull. They can put in a shunt and relieve the pressure. There is one test he wants to do to confirm that."

"So, what is the outlook?" asked Purah.

"He said it is possible that I can live a near normal life."

"Oh, that *is* good," said David. "You weren't normal before."

"Sorry for laughing, Ochre, but you deserve that," said Nathaniel.

That served to lighten the mood in the room as Gid began to lay aside his napkin and stand.

Nathaniel said, "Before y'all be goin', jus wanna remind y'all, we be havin Rosaneers tomorrow."

"I better bring my teeth," said David.

"LaMarah, have you heard that word before?" asked Purah.

"I had to think. Is it Roasting Ears or Corn on the Cob?"

Purah said, "Yes and you better bring your teeth."

They all laughed. Miller said, "Purah, it isn't likely to find you cracking jokes."

"Nathaniel, would you stir up some Red Eye Gravy while I am here? You guys just don't know—this food is a dying art," said LaMarah.

"LaMarah, if you ax for the moon, I will try to git it for ya," said Nathaniel.

CHAPTER THIRTY-TWO
Gideons Announce Their Move

"Purah and I have some news, also," said Gid.

David chimed in, "Are you having another baby?"

"I wish I could be lighthearted about this, but I have not wrapped my mind around it yet."

"Purah and I received a letter from the management. Our lease will not be renewed. Mrs. Morrison was correct in that having Charity Grace live here puts us out of compliance with the lease.

"At the present, we are praying about how to handle it. I asked God, 'Should we request a hearing?' He assured me he is bringing circumstances around for our good.

"Therefore, we are waiting."

"This is our dilemma too," stated Miller. "We know that God works all things for our good. We know how to pray."

"We are aware, we all came here to live close together. Please do not think we expect any of you to move. You all need the services here and are happy and settled.

"We will be able to find the help we need in conventional housing. We will be able to eat here anytime.

"We ask that you all pray that we find a suitable situation. We are looking at some possibilities.

"We have an appointment with a gentleman this afternoon about a good possibility.

"Oh, and by the way, I want you all to know, we have a special guest for dinner tonight. My friend Dr. Benjamin Solomon will be joining us."

Gid and Purah rushed off to their appointment.

"Daddy, Gid and Purah are such fascinating people. They have their way of loving everybody."

"LaMarah, I welcome this opportunity to get to know his doctor. Something about that man is intriguing," said Pansie.

#

"Matt, I so appreciate you making time for us, with such short notice," said Purah, as she and Gid arrived at Matt's office. "Your developments are always so appealing."

"Reverend and Mrs. Gideon, I am so glad you called. Come in and sit down."

Gid said, "Your secretary said you are in the early stages of a development that might interest us."

"That's right, sir." This might be the thing you are looking for."

"Matt, our circumstances are quite different than most people's. We are both seventy-seven years old. Don't get me wrong, we plan on living a long time. However, our needs are unusual. We have an adopted daughter and our lease where we currently live will not allow children to live there."

"You are losing your lease?"

"That's right, Matt. We will need all the handicap amenities but realize having a child in a neighborhood presents challenges at times.

"Where we live, our neighbors have been our friends since childhood. We are like family. They are in our home daily. What is more, they are all godparents to our daughter. Our first choice would be to keep those factors as a part of our living arrangement."

"You need a two-bedroom with ample family room?"

"Will there be a clubhouse?"

"Yes, sir, Reverend, a clubhouse and restaurant.

"Reverend and Mrs. Gideon, that really surprises me that they are not renewing your lease.

"My architect is currently drawing up plans for this new development. Let me get with him and relay your needs and concerns and see if we can come up with what you need."

"So, when are you looking to move?"

Gid's quick response, "We were given sixty days."

"That is a very tight timetable. Let's get together on Tuesday afternoon and maybe I can give you something concrete to go on."

As the Gideons were going out the door, Matt was already on the phone.

"I knew this development was needed in our little town, Ms. Lacey. Get our architect on the phone.

"Mitchell, what is a timeline for us to complete our first unit, with C.O. and everything?"

CHAPTER THIRTY-THREE
Dr. Solomon's Adoption

Dr. Solomon arrived at the Harbor Oaks Assisted Living dining room, moments before the Oaks. *Why am I so anxious?* Peering through the lattice, and glad he wasn't visible, *this must be LaMarah coming up the path with her mom and her dad on the scooter.*

He turned away as the door opened, with the Watkins chatting and heading into the dining area, not noticing him.

Exhaling in relief, *that was my Mother.* Walking toward the door now, "Reverend and Mrs. Gideon, I am grateful for the invitation this evening."

"Ben," said Gid, "we will just carry on with chitchat. Without putting LaMarah on the spot, you can tell them about your investigation. Let her play the next card. Keep in mind, this group is family. We have no secrets."

Walking into the dining room, "Nathaniel, what is on the menu tonight?"

"Unca Gid, I made your favorite tonight, Smoked Brisket and Buttermilk Pie."

"Nathaniel, I must say, with all our favorites, we have an interesting menu."

As everyone was gathering around the table, Gid remained standing. "Nathaniel, and friends, I want you all to meet my good friend, Benjamin Solomon. Ben was my Hospice doctor. I think he is still in disbelief about my improvement."

"Well, Mr. Ben, if you are Mr. Gid's friend, then you be mine," said Nathaniel.

"Ben, there isn't a more loyal friend in the world than Nathaniel," commented Purah.

Gid asked, "Miller, will you ask the Lord's blessing on our evening meal?"

As everyone was being seated, Charity Grace let her presence be known.

"Now Ochre, don't you give her the hiccups again," said Purah.

Laughing, Purah told Ben, "You have to be firm with Ochre."

"She wants me to. She was pulling at my mustache," said Ochre.

Introducing everyone, Gid saved the Watkins for last.

LaMarah said, "Ben, what is your specialty? Are you a geriatrician?"

"When I started my practice, I was as an internal medicine doctor, and found so many avenues of interest. I have a subspecialty in Hospice medicine, and medical geneticists."

"So how do you like being a medical geneticist?"

"Ms. LaMarah, that is a field that I have the most interest in at this time. You see, I am adopted, and I know virtually nothing about my birth parents, so I have questions about my own genetics."

LaMarah suddenly became uncomfortable with that turn of conversation.

Cutting her eyes at Gid, "Well, that makes perfect sense," she said.

Gid took the hint. "Ben, it looks like Purah and I will be moving."

"Gid? That is quite unexpected. I could see all the Oaks living here a lifetime."

"That was our hope, but we no longer meet the criteria to live here with a child under the age of eighteen.

"I will fill you in on the details as soon as we make a decision."

Nathaniel, proudly parading the beautifully decorated and garnished buttermilk pie to their table, "Who wants al a mode?"

Ben remarked, "No wonder you folks are all so healthy."

"Ochre, do you want ice cream?"

"No thanks, Nat, just put a little stogie on the side."

That was too much for David. Bursting out laughing, "Ochre, don't let the doc see your real self. You are supposed to be on good behavior."

"That *is* my good behavior. I could have come in here smoking one."

"David, did you grow up here in Harbor Oaks?"

"I certainly did. My dad had a general store. We lived upstairs in the store building. I went to school with the crew...I mean the Oaks.

"Our college years were the first time we had been separated. We all followed different tracks. Our teacher, Mr. Weeks, advised us to follow what we enjoyed and did well," said David. "I taught orchestration at the university."

"What about the rest of you? Purah?"

"I taught communication."

"And you, Dr. Morrison?"

"I served during WWII getting a doctorate in chemistry, and I am a medical doctor."

"Mrs. Morrison?"

"I pursued the legal profession. I was a trial lawyer."

"Pansie?"

"I was the athletic director for the university."

"Maude?"

"I spent my career as the county agent."

"Miller?"

"I was an animal scientist and the local veterinarian."

"And Ochre, I had to save you for last. You might steal the show."

"I can't steal the show. Scruffy is the show.

"I started out as a social worker and became the state director of DFS."

"So, it looks like you had your careers and retired back here in Harbor Oaks?"

"Oh, no," said Gid. "We managed our careers and never moved away. The ones of us who didn't work here, commuted. Our lives are so intertwined, we are like family."

"This is interesting. I imagine there are a lot of social dynamics going on in your group?"

Purah said, "The very fact that we are from a small town impacts our connections too. We have always gone to the same church, visited in one another's homes, and been there for one another during tragedies."

"And LaMarah?"

"Ben, my life has been vastly different. After college, I did not come back here, for personal reasons."

Ben's heart skipped a beat and he turned away, hiding the tears.

#

After dinner ended, the Oaks began to break up and head toward their apartments.

"Ruf, Ruf, Ruf, and Ruf, Ruf, Awf, Awful, Wafl. I said, Ruf, Ruf, Ruf."

"Ochre, I believe Scruffy needs you," said Miller.

Ochre, gladly slipping out with a piece of beef, "Scruffy, are you wanting my leftovers?" while wiping Scruffy's mouth with his dinner napkin.

"Mom," said LaMarah, "I am stopping by the Gideons on my way in."

Then LaMarah turns to Ben. "Ben, I would like to know more about your adoption. Do you think you can talk a while?"

"Certainly." Thinking*, and now my palms are sweating. I wish Desiree were here.*

#

While Purah got Charity Grace ready for bed, Gid, in his valiant fashion, injected the clincher. "LaMarah, Ben had shared a bit of his adoption with me, and my true purpose for his being here tonight was to meet you."

Seating herself beside Ben, feeling Gid wanted her to reassure Ben, she said, "Ben, how do you feel about your adoption?"

"LaMarah, I had parents who loved me and were good to me. I knew from my teenage years that I was adopted. I always felt there was some sort of void inside of me. I could not understand why. I still feel that."

LaMarah thought, *Should I go there?*

"Ben, I placed a baby boy for adoption while I was in college. It was the hardest thing I ever did. I knew there was a huge chance the State would take him from me, if I didn't voluntarily place him. A college student who was a single mom would have been under their magnifying glass.

"My college pastor and his wife had never had children. I allowed them to adopt my son. They would permit me to see him occasionally, just from a distance. I appreciated that so much. It helped me know he was healthy, loved, and well cared for."

After a long pause, "Ms. LaMarah," clearing his throat, he began slowly, "I believe *you* are *my* mother."

LaMarah began to weep, almost to the point of being inconsolable.

Purah came in and broke the intensity. "Gid, just let her cry. Tears are cleansing."

Purah said, "LaMarah, this is the day we have all prayed for. It is a day of enlightenment for both of you."

"Ben, your tears are quenching a longing that your heart could not express. God loves you both so much."

"Ben," LaMarah said while reaching for him, "our meeting this way must be God's plan. I did not want to disrupt your life, but I wanted so badly to see you."

Taking her head in his hands, and kissing her hair, "This had to happen, LaMarah."

Gid asked Ben, "Will you stay over with us tonight so you can have some time with Ochre and Pansie tomorrow?"

"Well, I certainly enjoy the pleasure of good company. It will be my pleasure, Reverend."

"LaMarah, let us all meet in the Grove tomorrow around 10 o'clock," said Gid.

"Sure thing. It will give me some time to prepare them. I have something else I need to take care of, before then."

#

First thing the next morning, LaMarah was at David's apartment.

"Well come in, my dear. What brings you over here?"

David's apartment was furnished in period Victorian, with wool rugs and hurricane lamps. The seating all faced the picture window, with the river park in view.

"David, it is past the time I should have this conversation with you."

Puzzled, "Is there a problem? Have a seat, LaMarah."

Trying to get comfortable in the chair, then walking over to Davie's overturned picture, on the table, "You were with us in the park, when I told everyone about my unplanned pregnancy and the adoption," she said.

"There were so many reasons I couldn't abort that baby, David. Everyone believes that the baby was Mark's.

"We were too involved for sure, but I know you remember how Davie had a crush on me. He carried my books to class, he bought me gifts, and would walk me home."

Sitting again, "Mark and I were fighting."

"David…, Davie was trying to console me, and we let it go too far. Davie never knew I was pregnant with his baby."

"LaMarah, I don't know what to say."

"Dad and Mom thought an abortion would fix the whole problem. They never knew the baby was Davie's.

"I was carrying so much guilt already, but I just couldn't abort that baby. You remember, I went away to college and broke all ties with my family."

"Well, yes, I do remember."

"And, you now know, I gave my little boy up for adoption. I was so miserable. My life had become a big lie, and still my family did not know the rest of the story.

"After all these years, my son and I have reunited. It was quite a coincidence."

"How did it all come about?"

"David, he was Gid's Hospice doctor, Ben Solomon."

Stroking his pencil-style mustache, "So that clarifies the mystery of why Gid brought him to dinner.

"LaMarah, I am feeling pretty numb. This is a lot for me to grasp. So, you say, Davie never knew about the baby?"

"I guess I should have told him. Knowing would only have made him miserable. I assumed all the blame for what happened.

"When I heard that Davie drowned, I was thankful he didn't know. We would have all believed; the drowning was not an accident," said LaMarah.

"So, Ben stayed the night with the Gideons. You will have an opportunity today to talk to him," she said.

"Reverend Gideon and Purah have known about this convoluted mess from the beginning, but not about Davie. He counseled me through every step. There is a lot of advice I should have taken. They will meet us in the grove, at 10 o'clock, said LaMarah.

"LaMarah, I am thankful you finally told me, and I will know him as my grandson. This gives me new perspective. For me, I am proud to know I have a grandson."

David was weeping now. "LaMarah, I don't have anyone except the Oaks. I will see you, dear, in the Grove."

As LaMarah left David's, she saw him turn Davie's picture back over.

CHAPTER THIRTY-FOUR
The Anchor

Gid and Ben stood on the riverbank watching the ships being guided by the tugboats.

"Ben, the smells and sounds of river life have their own personality. There is a new lesson out here every day.

"I believe you are a deep thinker, Ben. My teaching frequently contains word pictures from my childhood as a river rat on this riverbank."

"Reverend, that is interesting. Just what do you mean?"

"'Look at the ships,'" quoted Gid, "'though they are so great and are driven by strong winds, are still directed by a very small rudder wherever the inclination of the pilot desires. So also, the tongue is a small part of the body, and yet it boasts of great things. See how great a forest is set aflame by such a small fire. And the tongue is fire the very world of iniquity, the tongue is set among our members as that which defiles the entire body, and sets on fire the course of our life, and is set on fire by hell' James 3:4-6."[56]

"Reverend, that is amazing. It leaves an abiding impression."

---

[56] ((NASB) n.d.)

"You see, Ben, preaching is delivery of sermon. There are many styles. Jesus used several styles himself. He used true stories, parables, hyperbole. He would ask questions, and one of my favorites was object lessons. The purpose of it all is to share the depth of Jesus' love for us. It was a sacrificial love that demands a response."

"Reverend Gideon, I grew up in church. My takeaway, 'Try to be good.'"

"Ah, Ben. We can never be good enough. That was the teaching of the Old Testament and the animal sacrifice system. They had the laws they could not keep. The high priest had to offer the blood from the animal sacrifices for sin every year. When you understand that, you understand why there had to be a more perfect sacrifice spoken of in Hebrews.

"Scripture tells us:

For such an high priest became us, who is holy, harmless, undefiled, separate from sinners, and made higher than the heavens;
Who needeth not daily, as those high priests, to offer up sacrifice, first for his own sins, and then for the people's: for this he did once, when he offered up himself. (Heb 7:26-27)[57]

"It comes down to the simple facts: We sin; we need a savior. We cannot be good enough. It takes the grace of God to provide mercy. It takes our belief in Jesus, the incarnate God, and his holy sacrifice for our sin."

"I believe there is a Jesus. Maybe I try to overthink this."

"Ben, Jesus went into the Holy of Holies in heaven, after His resurrection, offering His own blood for our sin. He was crucified on a cruel Roman cross.

---

[57] ((KJV) n.d.)

"Scripture teaches: 'But God commendeth his love toward us, in that, while we were yet sinners, Christ died for us' (Rom 5:8.)[58]

"Ben, I am sure you have noticed how Purah loves people. It is a genuine love, and people respond to it. They feel accepted. In a similar way, knowing the love of Jesus evokes a response.

"Your response is either to accept what he did for you or to reject it. It is that simple."

"Ben, what is your response?"

"Reverend Gideon, you have made it so plain." Ben stepped over and sat on the bench. "Anyone could understand it." He took out his handkerchief and began to weep. "I can't do anything but accept it. My heart tells me this is right, Reverend Gideon."

Gid sat down beside him. "Ben, this is what the Bible says about the anchor: 'Which hope we have as an anchor of the soul, both sure and steadfast, and which entereth into that within the veil' Heb 6:19.[59]

That anchor is inside the 'veil' or the 'Holy of Holies' where Jesus made that one-time sacrifice. Your soul is anchored in Jesus, Ben."

"Ben, I want you to say, 'My soul is anchored in Jesus.'"

Closing his eyes, with a big smile, Ben said, "My soul is anchored in Jesus."

#

"Dad, Mom, there is something we need to discuss before we go to the park," said LaMarah.

Ochre commented, "LaMarah, this is a fruitful visit."

---

[58] ((KJV) n.d.)
[59] ((KJV) n.d.)

"Well, I don't know how you will feel about that when I tell you this.

"Daddy, just stay seated."

"Mama, you better sit down too."

Pansie, easing into her chair, "Baby, is something wrong?"

"I guess you could say my visit last night at the Gideons happened to be productive."

"Ben stayed over. He wanted to talk about his adoption. Mama, Daddy, he told me he believes that I am his mother."

"Oh, Ochre, I am so thankful."

"LaMarah," said Pansie. "I am elated. How do you feel about that?"

Blotting tears welling in her eyes, "Everything seems to match. His birthdate and his backstory. I believe he is my son."

Ochre commented, "The timing of this is unbelievable."

"Ben told me he had an emptiness that nothing would satisfy. His wife encouraged him to do all he could to get answers.

"There is more. Remember, I mentioned in the park, Mark thought the baby was his. Truth is, he belonged to a thirteen-year-old. Mama, Daddy, that thirteen-year-old was Davie Adams."

"Davie! Ochre, did you know?" said Pansie.

"Mama, not even Davie knew. I was so glad he didn't know. I would have thought his drowning was not an accident."

Making a deep sigh, Pansie asked, "Have you told David?"

"I told him this morning. I didn't know how he would take it. He seemed incredibly happy to have a grandson and hoped that he might be able to know Ben.

"Mama, Daddy, David has nobody but you guys. It is so sad.

"This is just one more way Reverend Gideon helped our family. He arranged the meeting with Ben.

"God brought Ben to Reverend Gideon so that I could know my son."

Ochre said, "I believe all this came about because we were able to forgive those who have hurt us. God redeemed our family. Oh, wow! I can hardly comprehend this."

#

As LaMarah walked down the path, she fixed her eyes on Ben. "Ben, there is more to the story that you don't know."

"I am in hopes of getting more answers today," Ben said. "The one foremost in my mind is: Who is my father?"

"You really need to know this, but I am so ashamed to tell you."

"What can it be? I imagine it is just part of a situation that prompted my adoption."

"Ben, it is shameful for me, for more than one reason. For one, I was pregnant out of wedlock. The worst part of it, Ben, the father was a thirteen-year-old boy who had a crush on me.

"God is redeeming our mistakes, though. The David that you met last night would be your grandfather. His son Davie drowned a few years ago. David's wife is deceased. You are David's only kin."

"LaMarah, I've got to sit down. On my normal day, I am used to being in control of situations. I view everything objectively.

"I think I am on information overload. I guess I wasn't expecting this many puzzle pieces—all at one time."

Everyone was gathering in Harbor Oaks River Park, as Nathaniel was wheeling the cart down the path to the tables.

As the path wound around the whitewashed trees, you could see David with his flute. Abruptly stopping, he purposefully made longer strides to LaMarah and Ben.

LaMarah, placing her hand on David's forearm, "David, I want you to meet Dr. Benjamin Solomon."

"Dr, Solomon, it is truly my pleasure."

"Dr. Solomon, I want you to officially meet your grandfather, David Adams."

Standing, Ben reached for his hand.

David's eyes were a little more than moist. "Ben, it is my honor and pleasure to meet you. I can see the resemblance you bear to my son. You have his beautiful brown eyes and energetic smile. My heart is about to explode. God is so good."

"Yes, He favored us here today," said Ben.

Ben, reaching for Reverend Gideon, "Before we go any further with this," said Ben, "I want to thank Reverend Gideon for orchestrating all of this for us. More than anything, I want to thank him for guiding me into a relationship with Jesus, the Anchor of my soul, just today."

Tears flowing down Miller's face, he stood—waving his frail arms. "Praise you, Jesus."

LaMarah said, "I just don't know what else can happen to make this any better."

After a bit of celebration, LaMarah said, "Mom and Dad, we discussed last night that Ben is my son I placed for adoption thirty-five years ago."

Ben reached for them both. Embracing one another, Pansie commented, "Ben, I can't take my eyes off you. I never thought I would see this day."

"I will want you all to meet my wife," Ben said. "If I had known all this would have transpired, she would have been here."

Nathaniel was elated. "Ochre, you done got yo fambly back, and David, you got yoself a fambly.

"David, you and Ochre got mo to fight over now than ever."

CHAPTER THIRTY-FIVE
Dudley's Disease

With the Taylor siblings being a part of the scenario, there was never a dull moment.

Papa was fascinated with their abilities and opportunities they were afforded.

"Rosie would be so proud of these kids," Dudley said. "We were never able to afford sports or training for 'em. Now, their week is all about Wednesdays.

"Reverend, I don't know how to tell ya this. Guess I'll just say it. I got liver disease."

Gid took him by the elbow and walked him over to the bench. Dudley never had a handkerchief; the tears were streaming.

"Reverend, I'm a sick man."

Gid pulled his bed-sheet-sized handkerchief out and handed it to him.

"My doctor tells me I'm, uh, dyin."

"Dudley, what happened?"

"I been drinking all these years. I am sober now, but it is just too late."

"Dudley, you are a young man. How long you got?"

"My doctor didn't tell me. He just said I needed to get my business in order."

"Is there any chance for a transplant?"

"Reverend." Dudley stopped to blow his nose, "I don't know what kinda questions to ask."

"Listen, Dudley, I want to go with you to your next doctor appointment."

#

Dudley was declining day by day.

#

"Dr. Lucas, this is my friend Reverend Gideon."

"Yes, I believe I know the Reverend."

"Doc, I wanted to come to Dudley's appointment today to fully understand his diagnosis."

"Reverend, I am glad you are here. Mr. Taylor needs a friend right now.

"Mr. Taylor," said Dr. Lucas, "Your cirrhosis is well advanced. There is extreme damage to your blood vessels and kidneys."

"Doc Lucas, we were hoping he would be a candidate for a liver transplant."

"Dudley, I am referring you to a liver specialist. He will be able to answer your questions. My office will make your appointment. They will be calling you back soon."

"And Reverend Gideon, *your* recovery is truly remarkable. You look like a much younger man."

Gid gave a big belly laugh. "Dr. Lucas, that little girl keeps me young. Her needs exceed my own. We don't have time to grow old. God knew I needed healing, for the excellence Charity Grace deserves, to take root in her life.

"Doc, Dudley here is her biological father with nine other children at home. This diagnosis is grim news, to say the least. We have put it in the hands of the Great Physician."

Shaking hands as they left, Doc Lucas said, "Fellas, I hope you can get some good news. Mr. Taylor, you couldn't have better friends at a time like this."

Dr. Lucas took Gid aside as they were leaving, "Reverend Gideon, there really isn't much hope. This has come from years of abuse."

#

"What am I going to do? My kids need me, Reverend," said Dudley.

Gid's thoughts were swirling around in his head.

Lord, what can I do to help him? What do we need to do next?

Gid said, "Do you have any people?"

"I have a sister. She has three kids of her own."

"Listen, Dudley. Our Oaks will meet in the morning for prayer. We will put you on the top of the list. This is as much about those children as it is about you."

CHAPTER THIRTY-SIX
Dudley's Decline

Dr. Lucas' office was able to get Dudley worked in for an emergency appointment with a hepatologist.

"Good morning, Mr. Taylor, I am your liver specialist, Dr. Daniel," speaking with a speech impediment.

Dr. Daniel was a preppy looking older man a with a full head of spiky short gray hair. He was frail in stature, with bow tie, plaid vest, and long sleeve white shirt.

"We are going to do a work-up on you that involves bloodwork, CT scans of your liver, kidneys, and abdomen. Today, we will do an ultrasound in the office and schedule you for a liver biopsy. That will give us valuable information," Mr. Taylor.

"Doc, will I be able to get a liver transplant?"

Hesitating, "Mr. Taylor, there are many variables that are involved in a diagnosis. Then we will determine what stage you are in. After I review your tests, I can give you a better answer. I am sorry. This is not a simple process.

"Mr. Taylor, the nurse will carry you down to the ultrasound tech. I will discuss the findings with you at your next appointment. I want to see you in one week."

#

"I can't make him hear me," said Gid, under his breath.

Looking through the screen, "Dud, are you ready for the appointment?"

Slowly walking in. "Dud, are you ready?"

"Help…help me," said Dudley.

"Sounds like he is in the bathroom. Dud, open the door."

Bam, bam, bam.

Gid could hear him on the floor.

"I can't get the door open, Dud. I will have to get help. Hold on, buddy."

Gid could hear the siren. Motioning to the EMTs, "He is on the floor of the bathroom.

"You guys are well prepared. How often do you remove doors?"

"More often that you think, Reverend. Step back, please."

As they removed the door, Dud's motionless body became visible.

Gid fell on his knees and scooped Dud up and began crying like a baby. Shaking his shoulders, "Dud, you can't go."

The EMT's knew he was gone. Giving Gid time, they walked onto the porch.

Coming back inside, "Are you family?"

"No, sir. Just a friend."

"I know who you are, Reverend. You were my boy's little league coach.

"Reverend Gideon, do you know any next of kin?"

Running his fingers through his hair. "Uh, yeah. We talked about that.

Gid said, "Guys, he has nine children, all in school, and his wife is dead. Tell me what to do."

"We'll have the coroner on his way. Meet us at the hospital."

By the time they arrived at the hospital, DFS was waiting.

Ms. Vermillia said, "Reverend Gideon, what happened?"

"Liver, I guess."

Turning her head away, biting her lips, "This is so sad, Reverend Gideon. All those poor children. Any other next of kin?"

"His sister, with three children of her own. It looks like your services will be needed, ma'am. I will give you his sister's contact information.

"The children had all left for school when I arrived, to pick him up."

Vermillia said, "That will give me some time. Thank you, Reverend Gideon."

"Let me know what we can do, Ms. Vermillia. We have been doing some training with the children. They are comfortable with us."

"I will get back with you, Reverend."

#

Ochre, out for his morning walk, "What happened, Gid? Why are you back so early? What happened?"

"My mind is in overdrive. I just found Dudley on his bathroom floor. He was wedged behind the door."

"How did you get him out? Was he okay?"

"It was too late, Ochre. The EMTs believed he may have hemorrhaged."

"So, what does all this mean? What can we do?"

"Ms. Vermillia was at the hospital when I left, I let her know we are available. You know, for the children."

"Ochre, will you get all the Oaks over right after lunch? We need to talk."

#

Pansie said, "This day started off bad. The headlines this morning was showing where the Murrow building in Oklahoma City was bombed. A daycare was in that building. Oh, but I am hopeful about the peace talks going on now between Syria and Israel."

Ochre filled everyone in on Gid finding Dud Taylor.

"Miller, will you start us off in prayer?

"Thank you, Miller."

"We need guidance," said Gid. "Some days, we might be better off in bed. We don't know when our feet hit the floor what we are facing. DFS arranged emergency foster care for the Taylor children, with Dudley Taylor's passing this morning."

"The floor is open for discussion. Anyone with any ideas?

"Yes, Mrs. Morrison."

"I don't feel we can abandon them now. There must be something we can do."

"I see nods of agreement throughout the room," said Gid. "We have prayed for guidance. If you believe we need to be involved in this, another battle, let's all continue to pray and wait to hear from Ms. Vermillia."

David said, "Ben will be here for a violin lesson this afternoon. I will see if he has any input."

"This is all in God's timing. As you all know, we will be moving tomorrow," said Gid. We have plenty of good help."

CHAPTER THIRTY-SEVEN
Cousin Gladys

The Gideons were the first to move into the new garden homes, on the knoll across from Fish Milk Holler.

"Oh, Purah, I am sorry," said Maude." I forgot about these mosquitos. I will get with Matt and work out a landscaping plan for the development. Certain plants will take care of those creatures."

"What? So, you know how to create that?"

"I certainly do. Those are the types of things I taught as an extension agent."

"Maude, I want to be able to spend as much time out of doors as possible," said Purah. "All the walking with Charity Grace is good for my back."

"Purah, Miller and I are moving over here too. We can still get the help we need and have an area for a container garden."

#

A lot of activity was going on with the Gideons' move. The Oaks were all coming and going.

Dr. Morrison walking out on the patio with Matt. "Thank you, Matt, for showing us the model last week. We have made our decision.

We will be giving our notice at Harbor Oaks Assisted Living. When will our unit be available?"

"It will be finished and landscaped in a month. You have made your decision at a good time. You will be able to pick out countertops, light fixtures, and paint colors."

"I will give you the deposit today and get things underway."

#

Maude whispered, "Oh, Purah, did you hear that? Did you expect that we would all move over here? Our biggest hurdle now is our food. Do you think Nathaniel will still let us go over for meals? I just can't survive without those cat-head biscuits."

"Maude, my heart is so full, LaMarah is moving back here," said Pansie. She can work from home some and will be able to take a commuter flight when needed. They have bought one of the apartments."

One by one, the other Oaks quickly followed suit. They hired a personal attendant to provide their housekeeping and assistance with their ADLs.

#

Soon after Ochre and Pansie got settled, he got a call from the sheriff.

"Ochre, we need to update you on the outcome of our findings in the well. I called to set up a meeting."

"Sure, come over to our new apartment. I will have all the Oaks here."

#

"Gid, this will be the final piece for my closure," said Ochre. "I have disposed of the property now and there won't be anything else to dispose of."

"Oh, I see the sheriff coming through the Holler," said Ochre.

"Come in, Sheriff Hunt."

Ochre said, "I believe you know all our Oaks?"

"I certainly do. It is my pleasure this morning."

"Sheriff Hunt sit here facing this window. The old cabin was down in that holler."

"Ochre, we are wrapping up our investigation, so I wanted to fill you in on everything."

"First of all, the bone that Reverend Gideon discovered was that of a Ms. Gladys Watkins."

"Whaaaat?"

"Yes, this was a cold case from back in the 1920s," said Sheriff Hunt.

"Ms. Gladys was charged with the murder of Mrs. Annabelle Watkins. It seems Gladys disappeared and was never brought to trial. We learned from you that the house had been closed since Ms. Annie passed, and it remained vacant. Apparently, Gladys hid in the well when they came to arrest her. For some unknown reason, she died in the well."

"I am astonished. How would anyone *ever* have known she met her demise. I guess justice was served," said Ochre.

"Yes, but there is more."

"More?"

"Yes, more. Perhaps you can shed some light on this one, Ochre."

"Because human bones were found in the well, it had to be cleaned out. There were four badly oxidized buckets in the well, like the lard buckets back then. The tops were on them, and inside each was the remains of a fetus."

"Oh, my."

Ochre was obviously disturbed. "That was my recurring dream. Oh, how disgusting."

It took Ochre a moment to regain his composure.

"Sheriff Hunt, in my dream, Cousin Gladys gave me a bucket to put in the hole. It was so vague in my dream; I didn't know if it was a memory or a dream."

"Apparently, Ochre, your mother gave birth to twins that day, but the other fetuses?"

Ochre studying, then silent. "I feel sick. Hum. I was told Cousin Gladys was a midwife. So, the mystery remains. Given her behavior, were the babies stillborn, or were they, uh, wasted?" said Ochre.

Gid said, "Ochre, her disappearance and lack of trial could be much of the reason you never knew anything. There wasn't any conclusion to the whole enigma."

"I will arrange to bury their remains, Sheriff. This is a most unexpected outcome, but it answers so many questions. At last, I can close this chapter of my life."

Ochre, reaching for the sheriff's hand, "I appreciate your stopping by.

"I do have a couple of questions. According to the gossip column from those days," said Ochre, "Gladys poisoned Mama with fish milk poison. You may not know the answer. Did Fish Milk Creek get named from fish milk poison?"

"Ochre, I am sorry, I just can't tell you."

"Ochre, if anyone would know that it would be Gordon Pollard. He is in the nursing home over on the hill. Let's pay him a visit tomorrow," said Gid.

"Gordon Pollard is Snitch, right? You don't mean he is still alive?"

CHAPTER THIRTY-EIGHT
Whitewashing and Grafting Trees

"Mrs. Waits, you probably remember me. I am Chuck Converse from Lighthouse Encounter Broadcasting and this is Chris our cameraman.

"I apologize for just dropping by. I didn't have your phone number."

"I certainly do remember you, Chuck. Please come in. Won't you have a glass of iced sweet tea with mint? I grow the mint in my little herb garden.

"Would you care for some, Chris?"

"Mrs. Waits, that would be a special treat. I am a fan of this southern hospitality, with the sweet tea, biscuits and gravy, grits, and even cornbread."

"We are so proud to offer kindness to our guests."

Chuck said, "Ms. Maude, It seems our community just can't get enough of the Parenting Paradox. You are such a part of Charity Grace's life; we are requesting an interview with you."

"It will be my pleasure, boys."

#

"Aunt Maude, Aunt Maude," running inside, "they have white brushy things."

"Charity Grace, that is the city workers."

"What are they doing, Aunt Maude?"

"Land sakes, what will they do next around here? It looks like they are whitewashing the trees," said Maude.

"Can you blue wash trees?"

"I suppose you could," said Maude.

"I want to help them."

"Those men are working; we wouldn't want to be in their way."

"Why are they doing that?"

"You stand here and watch them through the door, baby."

"Excuse me, Mr. Converse, every experience for her is a teaching opportunity."

"Maude, that is precisely why I am here. I will start taping if you don't mind."

Chuck began, "Once again, we are here at Harbor Oaks Assisted Living in our quest to understand the Parenting Paradox. One of the Oaks, Maude Waits' instruction for Charity Grace gives her an agricultural facet to her education. Now, Mrs. Waits is a retired county extension agent.

"Today it seems, Charity Grace is learning about 'whitewashing' trees."

"Ms. Maude, please continue your description of whitewashing."

"Whitewash is lime, Charity Grace. It comes in powder form and you mix it with water. It is applied with a brush in much the same way you apply paint. They apply it every year to protect the bark of trees, especially fruit trees. It prevents damage from insects and cold."

"And what is more, it's a nice aesthetic effect, and it is becoming quite fashionable," remarked Maude.

"What is aesthetic?"

"The trees look neat and clean. It is simple and nice."

Then Chuck asks, "So, Ms. Maude, do you mind if I call you Ms. Maude? You retired as county extension agent. Am I correct?"

"Yes, my job was in agriculture production, along with animal science marketing and fieldwork with the 4-H[60] students."

"You see, Charity Grace, whitewashing can infer a lot of different things. Some people use that term when they say you are living above your raising or trying to cover up something," said Maude.

Chuck's eyes widened. He said, "Yes, I have heard that used in a derogatory way."

"Some folks try to put a handle on everything," she said. "In their minds, it must be one way or the other. My grandmother was a slave-daughter of a white man. I am a mixture of Irish, African, British, and Scotch-Irish. Now, I married a Caucasian, so some folks would say I am trying to be whitewashed."

"Our friends here in Harbor Oaks don't see ethnicity. They look at your heart. They look at how you treat other people.

"This little community came a long way in my lifetime. We had a schoolteacher who taught us that God created every living being. Human beings are created in the image of God. We learned we are equal in God's economy.

---

[60] ([4-H Club])

"Our parents and grandparents had a different understanding of that, but with us needing to depend on one another during the Depression, we experienced unforgettable connections that endeared us to one another.

"You see, Mr. Converse, our crew we call the Oaks is a unique group, and we know it. We prayed for God to allow us to continue to preserve our legacy in a meaningful way. That is what this Parenting Paradox is all about. We are passing our baton to Charity Grace. Our *Closing Life-Challenge* involves living with a different perspective, yielding a Biblical Model of love."

"Maude, would you describe that Biblical Model?"

"Obviously, it is Love.

"We are vessels and then instruments of God's love."

Chuck asked, "how is that fleshed out, or how does God use us as His instruments?"

"He was speaking of grafting a wild vine into a cultivated vine. He specifically spoke of grafting the Gentile vine into the Jew root. That would be a spiritual adoption. This person experiences a new birth.

"Jesus taught the principle of grafting: 'And if some of the branches be broken off, and thou, being a wild olive tree, were grafted in among them, and with them partakest of the root and fatness of the olive tree' Rom 12:17.[61]

"Our teacher Mr. Weeks taught us about grafting and how important it is to use a desirable root stock. Knowing that enables us to understand our relationship with our father, God.

Our spiritual root is none other than Jesus. The root of David, the Lion of the tribe of Judah.

---

[61] ((KJV) n.d.)

"Divine protection and purpose were evidenced by Moses being adopted by Pharaoh's daughter.

"Samuel's adoption enabled his mother to be involved in his life, as God prepared him to be a judge, warrior, priest, and prophet."

"Maude, how does that apply to Charity Grace?"

"Being adopted as a Gideon gives her all the legal benefits. God's plan for her life will unfold as she grows. For us, being God's instruments, or his hands, we will all be lovingly pouring ourselves into her, for as long as we live. Each of us is different, with many talents and spiritual gifts. We are endowing her with a many-faceted legacy that will yield a destiny that only God knows."

"Let us camp out here just a moment," Chuck said. "You mentioned, you would pour yourselves into her for as long as you live. It is a given, you are all advanced in years. Correct me if I am wrong. You are all in your seventies."

"Closer to eighty, but to answer your question, yes, we as God's instruments pour ourselves into her, our vessel.

"We know our limitations, Chuck. We know they mostly revolve around our age. Our comfort comes from knowing we are to "occupy until He returns' Lu 19:13,[62] as Luke the Physician taught us."

"Oh, you mean Dr. Lucas?"

"Luke was a physician in the New Testament who recorded the events in Jesus' day."

As the camera panned to Chuck, "Join us next week as we learn more about Charity Grace's progress in the Parenting Paradox. I believe I am seeing a common thread in this group of Oaks that is leading to this *Closing Life-Challenge.*

---

[62] ((KJV) n.d.)

"Ms. Maude, I feel I am richer, from just having met you. Each of you Oaks have intriguing lives to share.

"Our viewers are pressing us for more stories. The accounts you are all giving of your own childhood and the way you share them with Charity Grace are being met with great interest."

Maude said, "Yes Chuck, a three-fold cord is not easily broken." Ecc 4:12.[63]

"Viewers, what do you think Ms. Maude meant about a three-fold cord?"

---

[63] ((KJV) n.d.)

CHAPTER THIRTY-NINE
The Oaks meet Desiree.

Pansie and Purah were seated in front of the big picture window at the Gideons'.

"Pansie, I am feeling as though my retirement is over," said Purah. "We have the meeting with DFS today about the Taylor children. If God puts an adoption plan in place for us at our age, with Charity Grace, then he can create an amazing plan for the parenting of those sweet children."

"Who could that be at the door?" said Maude.

"Are you expecting anyone, Purah?"

"Come in, Ben. It is so good to see you."

"Gid and Purah, forgive me for just dropping by. I want you to meet my wife, Desiree."

The surprise meeting brought hugs for everyone, with Pansie's arm wrapped around Ben's waist.

Purah immediately engaged with Desiree in conversation.

Ben and Desiree met in graduate school. She was working on her Speech Therapy degree and neither of them had romantic interests in the beginning. They had a couple of classes together and met for lunch in the cafeteria. He fell in love with her passion and drive but tried to focus on his studies. She seemed to complete him in so many ways. He struggled to understand that kind of relationship.

Desiree always had a list of what she was looking for in her husband, and he met every detail.

"Mrs. Gideon, Ben is ecstatic since he met his mom, and then grandparents. He told me all about the Oaks."

"Desiree, you must have an interesting life. Tell me what you do to keep yourself busy."

Ben and Gid carried out some small talk and quickly got to the point of the visit.

"Reverend Gideon, Purah, please tell me what you know about the foster care of the Taylor children. Desiree and I cannot get them off our mind. The thought came to both of us about fostering them. We all know the best thing for them is to be in the same home. I kept stuffing the thought, and it kept coming back."

Desiree said, "Yes, we decided to talk about how we felt we could carry it out. The more we talked, the more possible it seemed. Difficult scenarios and logistical problems were explored. We understand the difficulties but Gid, God prepared us for this."

"So, Desiree and I feel we are being led into *this* 'Parenting Paradox.'

"What do you think, Gid?"

"God is bringing together a whole fleet of nurturers.

"God's timing is perfect. You two certainly seem to understand the weight of this endeavor. I am meeting with DFS today. Perhaps the two of you can attend."

#

Gid introduced Ben and Desiree to Weldon and Vermillia.

Shaking his head, after some lengthy conversation, Weldon said, "The department will agree to place the children temporarily with you, Dr. and Mrs. Solomon.

"Do you live in this county?"

"Yes, about ten miles away."

"We will waive the foster training, temporarily, in lieu of your medical training, Dr, Solomon.

"There are guidelines for sleeping arrangements that must be met.

"Our social worker will walk you through everything. Placement will be expedited for this emergency."

Ben accompanied them to the door. "Weldon, Vermillia, it is a pleasure to meet you. I look forward to working with your department."

Vermillia said to the Solomons, "I am hoping this arrangement works as well for the Taylor siblings as for Charity Grace.

"Gid, I am assuming the siblings will be able to continue their lessons and training with the Oaks."

"Ms. Vermillia, let me assure you, their welfare is as important to us now as before."

DFS workers seem relieved as they were leaving. Vermillia commented, "Placing these children in the same home is a Godsend, for them."

#

"Purah, Chuck is setting up an opportunity to update the viewers about this Parenting Paradox. He will be here at our apartment at 2, said Gid."

"Chuck, please come in."

"Reverend Gideon, I have been hearing about the Garden Apartments in Fish Milk Holler."

"They aren't really in the holler, Chuck. You drove through the holler to get up here on the knoll that looks down into the holler in the front, and across to the Harbor Oaks River Park in the side. Our view of the sunset across the river and through those trees is amazing."

"As we drove in, we got some clips of the holler. We will seat you on the patio to get a view of the Harbor Oaks in the background," said Chuck.

Chris, the cameraman zoomed in on Chuck, with a rolling motion of his hand.

"Here we are at the Gideons' new home in Fish Milk Holler. We have some updates on the Parenting Paradox," said Chuck.

"Reverend Gideon, there is a rumor that all the Oaks have moved here. Is that true?"

"Oh, yes. Some of us...hehehe...are frail elderly, but we are not living a dependent lifestyle. We are taking advantage of the benefits in the Homeowners Association."

"So, tell our viewers about Charity Grace's siblings."

"After the adoption was finalized," said Gid, "we felt strongly that Charity Grace's siblings needed contact and interaction with her and she with them. We designed a schedule one day a week for them to come over."

"Before we knew it, we were engrossed in teaching them, just as we do her. They were getting music lessons, riding lessons, golf lessons, and tutoring in law and science. They are an eager group."

"So, what happened next?"

"Their father passed unexpectedly, and we continued our relationship with them, fostering them for a short while.

"A medical doctor and his wife have taken the helm. They fostered them for a while but have now adopted all nine of them. This was one of those things that only God could have put together."

"Reverend Gideon, how do you explain the way this all came about?"

"This is something that requires meditating and study. Our souls, or rather the Oaks' souls, are 'anchored.' If you want to understand, study Heb 6:19."[64]

The camera panned back to Chuck.

"I hear someone singing outside. There is always something interesting going on with this group of folks," said Chuck.

As Gid looked out and saw Ben singing to the top of his lungs, Chris panned to the window "Oh, these are the adoptive parents coming up the walk, Chuck."

Ben robustly singing,

"I've anchored my soul in the Haven of Rest,
I'll sail the wide seas no more.

The tempest may sweep over wild, stormy deep.
In Jesus, I'm safe evermore."[65]

Reaching for Ben as he walked in the door, "Ben, I didn't know you sing."

"Oh yes, Gid. Singing out here is like singing in the shower. Love the echo. I have joined the choir. I am working on my solo."

"David needs to hear you soon."

---

[64] ((KJV) n.d.)
[65] (Gilmour 1885)

Chris panned again to Chuck. "We will continue this next week, to learn more about the so-called 'anchor of the soul' in this Parenting Paradox."

Viewers were calling in wanting to know more about the anchor. They had followed this story for years now, many not understanding the faith of the Oaks or the love they demonstrated.

CHAPTER FORTY
Snitch

It was surprising to learn that Snitch Pollard was still alive in the nursing home—what's more he had a fascinating view of Mosquito Fjord, the holler, and Fish Milk Creek.

It was puzzling to look at him. His appearance was of a much younger man, although he was bedridden, he was lanky but not at all frail. Bitter memories and cliffhanger tales were his companion,

"You fellars come in. I don't have many visitors. I have outlived all my folks except my son."

"Gordon," said Gid, "this is my friend Ochre Watkins."

"Oh, Ochre, I know who you are. I guess I know why y'all are paying me a visit."

Ochre said, "Gordon, I am an old man, but there are some things I have never known about my mother's death."

"So, I remember it, Ochre—lak yesterday! You see, Annabelle Watkins was my half-sister."

Ochre's eyes grew wide, and his head nodded back like he had been slapped. "Gordon, why didn't we ever know you?"

"I'll let you decide."

"That fancy smellin' Gladys came to town and acted like she owned the place. Said she was a midwife, so she was going to bring the Watkins baby into the world and help Annie for a while."

Ochre said, "We read the newspaper articles Snitch, so we know she poisoned Mama."

"That she did. She came to the tavern bragging about it that night. Course she had too much shine to drink and was spilling her guts. She told about the fish milk poison and killing the twin. Said she weren't taking keer of two babies."

In astonishment, Ochre said, "That was Woody's twin in the bucket she gave me to throw in the hole. That sickens me to think about it."

"Y're right. Not only did she kilt him, but she also kilt the Timbrok baby. Said that woman had too many yunguns already. You could see how evil she was, and on top of that, she was plum stupid.

"Don't know why she picked me to talk to."

Ochre said, "We know about her trying to poison you and her getting found out."

Ocher asked, "When they went to arrest her, why couldn't they find her?"

Snitch leaned forward, like he was whispering. "Boys, if ye tell 'em I told ye this, I'll say ye lied."

Gid and Ochre leaned into Snitch like a couple of ten-year-olds listening to a ghost tale.

"She was done dead," said Old Snitch.

"I told you she was stupid. She never figured out why I didn't die from the fish milk soup.

"So, back at the tavern, she is drinking. I'm telling her they are going to arrest her, and she wanted *me* to hide her.

"I said to myself, *she is the meanest thing ever in this county.*

"So, I put rattlesnakes in the well at your Granny's house and told Gladys to hide in the well. Hehehe. I knew they wouldn't look there 'cause the house was closed-up tight.

"I have lived with that all these years. You fellars are the only ones I told. What they gonna do to me now?"

Disregarding his question, Gid said, "I guess what we wanted to know pales in all that."

"What else did you fellars want to know?"

Ochre asked, "Did Fish Milk Creek get its name from her poisoning Mama?"

"Fish milk poison was already in her bag of sorceries. She told us she was one of them thar herb doctors, but I say she was a witch doctor. The creek there just jogged her memory."

Ochre asked, "Did you get your nickname from turning her in?"

"Snitch?" Giving a good belly laugh, "No, I told you she was mean and stupid.

"I may be mean, boys, but I ain't stupid!

"I knew there was a chance she may have never been convicted. Sheriff didn't have an eyewitness.

"My conscious never bothered me. Lynch mobs were common in those days. I didn't see this was any different. Maybe that is why my room here faces that place. Do you think I need to repent, Preacher?"

"Snitch, maybe that is why you are still alive. Maybe He is giving you time to repent, or time before your judgment. I marvel every day at His mercy."

Ochre said, "Snitch, I have one more question or observation. If my mother was your sister, was Crazy Granny your mother?"

Snitch's eyes filled with tears. "Yeah, boys, my poor Maw never hurt nobody. Gladys shouldn't have blamed her."

"Gid," said Ochre, "Mrs. Morrison is right. This would make a good movie. I can't cry. I can't laugh. All I can do is shake my head. There was a lot this old boy didn't know.

"I feel numb and at the same time a relief."

Ochre said, "Mr. Pollard, I sure hope you have peace about all this. You have helped me when nobody else could. Maybe that is why you are still here. Thank you, Sir."

"Sir? I don't know if anybody has every called me Sir."

"Gid," said Ochre. Let's head home.

CHAPTER FORTY-ONE
Scoundrel Ochre

"Gid, let's stop here at the park. These trees remind me of your exhortation, 'Like a Tree.'"

Gid parked the car beside the whitewashed trees with the river in view. He could always envision that old ship in the distance.

"Gid, thank you for going with me to visit Snitch. Thank you for so many things. All those years you helped LaMarah, you have been her lifeline. We never knew you paid for her education. You have been a 'tree of righteousness' (Isaiah 61:3)[66] in our lives."

"Listen, Ochre, we have always been like family. I didn't lose anything by paying her education. She needed us. For me and Purah, abandoning her at a time like that would have changed our direction in life. It would have changed everything about who we are and what we teach."

"But I have been such a scoundrel, in effect, we abandoned her. That verse in Jeremiah 17:9 echoes in my head day and night.

---

[66] ((KJV) n.d.)

'The heart is deceitful above all things, and desperately wicked: who can know it?'[67]

"Gid, I don't have to tell you, desperate people do desperate things. I was on the verge of suicide when LaMarah called. I was headed to my skydiving accident.

"Then, the forgiveness sermon came in the wake of it all. That started me on a liberation journey. Forgiveness of others is a powerful means to personal peace."

"Ochre, some truths take a lifetime to learn."

"There is still one thing I need to confess to you. I don't know what we need to do."

Gid's eyes were fixed on the ship. He knew what was coming.

"Gid, I am Charity Grace's father."

(Silence.)

"Gid, say something. You're not acting surprised."

"Purah figured it out early on, Ochre."

"You never let on like you knew. I almost took my life over that."

"Ochre, truth will always prevail. Charity Grace needs to know when she is old enough to deal with it.

"Listen, Ochre, Pansie is the one you need to be talking to about this."

"Gid, she has forgiven me for countless things in our marriage. I don't know why she stays with me. I can't expect her to forgive me, but my spirit says I must ask."

---

[67] ((KJV) n.d.)

"Marriage is more than just an intimate bond, Ochre. Think of the roots of a tree. They often grow together where one tree gets its nourishment from the other. 'One flesh' (Eph 5:31)[68] is the best way to describe it. Pansie understands.

"You have drawn off her all these years, Ochre. This would be a good time to turn the tide in her favor. Be the man God has created you to be.

"Ochre, the weight you carry will disappear, the drifting will stop Ochre, it is time to drop anchor."

"You have never led me wrong, Gid. I am committed to making things right. I owe it to her, I owe it to LaMarah, I owe it to Charity Grace, and I owe it to God."

"Gid, mine and Miller's childhood was so similar," said Ochre. He has always seemed at peace with his life, and I allowed the effect of my childhood to fester and kept me in a toxic state—the contrast is obvious."

"Ochre, you have always had a choice. You both knew Jesus from an early age, but your choices in life have anchored you to instability.

"You heard me tell Snitch. God has shown his grace to him, by leaving him here this long. He is showing grace to you, Ochre. If you live, it is never too late to change directions. You did not allow your compass—the Holy Spirit, to guide you."

"Ochre, you have already made great strides in healing those you have hurt. God will allow you to begin bearing fruit."

Ochre slowly got out of the car and walked over to the catch-all. He flipped the half-smoked crutch of a cigarette into it.

---

[68] ((KJV) n.d.)

As he sat again in the car seat, Gid said, "Ochre did you ever need that anyway?"

Ochre said, "that's just one of many crutches. I will be disposing of more."

CHAPTER FORTY-TWO
School Begins.

"Charity Grace let's get your lunch ready for school. You want your first day to be a success."

"Mama, will my brothers and sisters be there?"

"Yes, Baby. The younger ones will. Your older siblings will be at the middle school and high school.

"Today is the day you have your golf lesson. Try to stay clean, so you don't have to change clothes when you come in.

"Now what is that white stuff on your face? It looks like whipped cream."

Gid wiped it off and smelled it. Laughing he asked, "Why do you have shave cream on your face?"

"I wanted to look my best for my first day of school, so I shaved."

Grinning, Purah rolled her eyes.

Gid continuing, "So, what else did you do?"

"Polished my new shoes."

Gid looked down and could not believe what he saw.

"Your new black and white Oxfords have white polish on the black. Is there a reason for this?"

"I whitewashed them. Aunt Maude said whitewash protects the tree."

"I think you needed help with that."

Ochre had slipped in and threw his head back, laughing out loud. "Charity Grace, we will ride my scooter to school."

"Baby girl," said Gid, "say your new Bible verse you memorized for us, before you leave. This finishes your memorization of Psalm 23:6. Our prayer for you, Charity Grace, is that 'goodness and mercy follow you all the days of your life,'"[69] said Gid.

"Purah, I believe she understands that Psalm. She knows what a shepherd is. Miller taught her all about sheep."

"I think so too. The way she says, 'The *Lord* is *my* shepherd' makes me believe that.[70]"

#

Then she was off to school with Ochre. "Hop on the back, Charity Grace. Put this flower in your hair. You can let the wind blow through your hair as we ride the riverfront path.

"Baby," said Ochre, "you know your Mama Rosie had a 'garland of Grace' (Prov. 4:9)[71] on her head."

---

[69] ((KJV) n.d.)
[70] (Ibid n.d.)
[71] ((NASB) n.d.)

CHAPTER FORTY-THREE
Anchored

Reverend Gideon was overjoyed at the thought of Ben's visit today.

Falling into his recliner beside the window, "Purah, with Charity Grace graduating Monday night, I already don't like thoughts of an empty nest. What do you think about us going for a drive?"

"We are easily amused," laughed Purah. "Do you think you can get back out of that recliner?"

Gid began rocking to and fro, to throw himself onto his feet. "I know, I know. My therapist said I will throw myself onto the floor doing this."

"Just so you know, I won't be much help getting you up, now scoot to the edge of your chair."

"I need to drive, Gid. We depended on Charity Grace too much to chauffer us around."

They looked at each other with mischief in their eyes. "This may be too much excitement for us," said Gid, with a hearty laugh.

Purah said, "We always start out by going by the River Park."

"Well, let's get going. It will be time for Ben, and we will still be talking about it."

Driving the little convertible, "Gid, I just love our small town, where we know everybody we pass. They are all waving."

"Purah, hehehe, they don't know us. They are all looking at that old couple passing by and wondering who let us out of the nursing home. Hahaha!"

"Just humor me, Gid."

"So, who do you think is sitting on the bench beside the whitewashed oaks? Purah, he loves this place as much as we do."

Ben saw them arrive and came over to help them out of the car. "Reverend, I am just sitting here reminiscing about the day I was saved."

"Gid, I have a mental image in my mind of an anchor. It goes with me everywhere I go. That song is my mantra."

"What song?" Gid asked. 'He Anchored My Soul in the Haven of Rest'?"[72]

"Exactly." Dropping his head, Ben began to cry. "Sorry, Gid."

"Reverend Gideon, this world needs more people like you and Purah. I can't begin to count the lives you have influenced, just since I have been privileged to know you.

"You have cared enough to get involved in people's lives. I personally know Desiree and I would still be floundering had it not been for you two. You were instrumental in my salvation and my birth. Your counsel to LaMarah gave me life."

---

[72] (Gilmour 1885)

"Ben, we are sitting here beside the whitewashed trees that I enjoy so much. It is just an outer garment. The Bible talks about whitewash."

"Matt 23:27[73] gives such a vivid example to help us understand hypocrisy. Let me put it this way, speaking to the *holy* men of that day, Jesus tells them their outward appearance would make people believe they were holy, but their beautiful bodies were just whitewashed tombs, hiding repulsive, filthy bones.

"Yes, Ben, the whitewash on these trees is just a garment. It is what is inside that matters. These whitewashed trees are beautiful, but they have a root system that is their anchor. That root system gives them stability and hydration. Those tiny roots bring in minerals for their nourishment, without which they could not survive.

"I have lived my life with the goal of giving people a root system that would help them withstand the storms in their lives. These stately trees wouldn't be anything without their root. Believe me, the first wind would topple them right over. They would be worthless. These trees are a hundred, maybe two hundred years old. The storm may break a limb, but it doesn't uproot the tree.

"Ben, we are all stately Oaks. We have a root as our anchor. Jesus tells us in the book of Rev 24:16b,[74] 'I am the root and the offspring of David.' That root is what anchors us. Our anchor is Jesus."

"Gid, you put everything in perspective. I take care of people who are sick. I take care of their body, or their garment. I believe God is telling me to teach them to nurture their root."

Gid slowly stood. Taking Purah's hand, they began to walk to the riverbank. Gid's eyes were fixed on something in the distance.

---

[73] ((KJV) author's paraphrase n.d.)
[74] ((KJV) n.d.)

"Ben, son, I am leaving the *legacy* with you today of teaching and living that example. A legacy doesn't carry any weight without an anchor. That Anchor is our hope. Our hope is anchored in Jesus."

CHAPTER FORTY-FOUR
The Baccalaureate

Celebrations are common in a pastor's family. Charity Grace's college graduation marked a victory of biblical proportion in her life, as well as all the Oaks.

"Purah, my mind could not comprehend *this* day. Many times, over the years I have looked forward to this. We always knew God would allow us to see it."

"Gid, we have made history in many ways. Adopting her set a new precedent. Our living this long set a precedent."

Purah said, "that must be Chuck at the door. Come in Chuck. We are so glad to see you."

Patting Chuck on his back, "Chuck, you are an old man now, hehehe," said Gid.

"Yeah, don't remind me, Gid."

"Reverend Gideon, this may be my last interview. Let us go out with some flare. I want to record a shot of you leaving your home, then we will film while you drive your convertible toward the park. I will get full frontal view as you are giving the charge in Charity Grace's Baccalaureate speech."

With tears welling in Chuck's eyes, "Reverend Gideon, I don't know if I will ever see you again. This Parenting Paradox is the most watched, ongoing news saga on our network. It is affecting countless lives. Personally, I am a changed man because of it. I always go home and start digging in the Bible for the concepts you mention. You have made life make sense for a lot of people, not to mention me."

"Chuck, all I wanted to do is glorify my Creator. I owe Him everything."

#

Leaves on the massive, whitewashed oaks were rustling with the cool breeze off the river, and the delicate fragrance of the lemon verbena drifting through the air.

Chuck began in a whispered tone. "Ladies and gentlemen, we have approached this evening with great anticipation. As Reverend Gideon slowly walks to the grandstand at Harbor Oaks Park, the crowd is giving him a standing ovation. Many here have followed this Parenting Paradox for most of their lives.

"Present are the Oaks along with their families, Dr., and Mrs. Benjamin Solomon with their family of nine adopted children, Nathaniel and the employees of Harbor Oaks Assisted Living, the staff of *Live Encounter News*, in addition to graduates of Charity Grace's class along with their friends and families.

"As the Reverend Gideon is stepping forward, we hear the bell tolling in the Zion Church. You remember that bell is from the Charity Grace—ship.

#

"My beloved friends:

I will address you tonight as Witnesses. God demonstrated great principles in your lives, with the *Closing Life-Challenge* being but one of them.

"*This* day is The Realization of the *Closing Life-Challenge*."

"Our prayers on *that* day were to invoke the Holy Spirit into the launch of this voyage that would take us into unknown waters.

"I bring you good news. Looking back, God honored that prayer, as He prepared our path and went before us all the way. His Holy Spirit was truly the wind in our sails, charting our path as we navigated through waters that were sometimes murky.

"Looking forward, by faith I see Him using all His resources to do the same for each of you. Witnesses, He is 'Alpha and Omega God' (Isaiah 21:6-7)[75]. His presence will go with you, His Power will go with you, His Grace will go with you...to the end.

"Witnesses, all of you have a calling on your life.

"The *Oaks of Righteousness* (Isaiah 61:3[76]) claim the victory in the battle given on *that* day in this very grove. That Our God would be glorified.

"Purah, would you read from Isaiah 61:3, please?"

To appoint unto them that mourn in Zion, to give unto them beauty for ashes, the oil of joy for mourning, the garment of praise for the spirit of heaviness; that they might be called trees of righteousness, the planting of the Lord, that he might be glorified.[77]

"Graduates, I charge you *this day* to nurture those planted by the LORD—for His Glory, those sprouts of righteousness, in *your* life.

"You, 'Oaks of Righteousness,' bear fruit! Be about doing—doing what God created you to do!

---

[75] ((KJV) n.d.)
[76] ((NASB) n.d.)
[77] (Ibid n.d.)

"Oh, it is a beautiful thing. It is a deep thing. Yes, it is an eternal thing!

"Charity Grace, your world to some would appear utopic.

"As the Phoenix, you have risen from ashes.

"Beauty for ashes from your Creator God, not at all what this world could expect.

"You personally and individually have become a Tree of Righteousness (Isaiah 61:3),[78] lifting the head of the grieving to the Glory of the LORD.

"Your parents are proud of you. Your faithfulness to the call of God will open doors to you. Doors you do not expect.

"Although you know his gentle leading, because you have experienced it so many times, you will be in awe of what He is doing in you and through you.

"He knows that you will remain humble, for He tries you frequently, and you will give Him the glory.

"Please know Charity Grace Gideon, your Mother and I love you with our whole heart, precious anointed one."

Stepping back from the podium, the Reverend Gideon gave the witnesses time for their applause and standing ovation. Now, he stood with upward, pointed, feeble hands, giving God the glory. As he stepped back to the microphone, the camera panned the crowd. Everyone was waving their white handkerchiefs and cheering.

The gentle breeze was gaining strength and with that, a shower of rain moved across the crowd. They immediately noticed—no one was wet. It was raining and no one was wet. They had never experienced anything like this. Their cheering continued.

---

[78] ((KJV) n.d.)

Leaning into the mic, in a feeble voice, "now, on *that* day".

The crowd quieted-yet still standing as Reverend Gideon began:

For I am now ready to be offered, and the time of my departure is at hand. I have fought a good fight, I have finished my course, I have kept the faith:

Henceforth there is laid up for me a crown of righteousness, which the Lord, the righteous judge, shall give me at that day: and not to me only, but unto all them also that love his appearing. 2 Tim 4:6-8.[79]

_____

[79] ((KJV) n.d.)

CHAPTER FORTY-FIVE
Charity Grace Epilogue

To the faithful witnesses,

You have discovered my life is an exceptional masterpiece.

My family of artists lovingly sculpted and refined as gold, every facet of my personality, my intellect, my character, and even my sense of humor.

I have been their medium, where they have applied brushstrokes, or sculpted, trained, and composed.

My heart bears the fruitful imprint of a sacrificial passion born out of gifted obedience to God.

I humbly accept this charge on my life today, to diligently apply these disciplines, in order to be useful to the Master.

In Christ alone,
Charity Grace Watkins-Taylor-Gideon,
PH.D., MD.

Author-Janice R. Hunt

#helpadoptionlegacy
#anchoredbook
#assistedliving
#assistedlivinghome
#bondwithadoptedchildren
#closinglifechallenge
#depressionyears
#faithhelp
#helpfaith
#furbaby
#helpforgiven
#forgiveness
#garlandofgrace
#Godusesweakness
#grace
#grafted

#grafting
#hanaiadoption
#havenofrest
#legacy
#legacyliving
#love
#makeafriend
#prayer
#psalm1
#righteousness
#southernappalachia
#scruffyfurbaby
#teachers
#theoaks
#treeofrighteousness
#whitewash

CPSIA information can be obtained
at www.ICGtesting.com
Printed in the USA
JSHW030218220521
15005JS00002B/5